Self-employment, Small Firms and Enterprise

PETER URWIN

iea
The Institute of Economic Affairs

First published in Great Britain in 2011 by
The Institute of Economic Affairs
2 Lord North Street
Westminster
London SW1P 3LB
in association with Profile Books Ltd

The mission of the Institute of Economic Affairs is to improve public understanding of the fundamental institutions of a free society, with particular reference to the role of markets in solving economic and social problems.

A CIP catalogue record for this book is available from the British Library.

ISBN 978 0 255 36610 6

Many IEA publications are translated into languages other than English or are reprinted. Permission to translate or to reprint should be sought from the Director General at the address above.

Typeset in Stone by MacGuru Ltd
info@macguru.org.uk

Printed and bound in Britain by Hobbs the Printers

Self-employment, Small Firms and Enterprise

CONTENTS

THE AUTHOR

Peter Urwin is director of the Centre for Employment Research and Professor of Applied Economics at the University of Westminster. He has focused on the application of approaches used primarily in the field of economics, across a wide variety of subjects. Peter has published in journals such as *Work, Employment and Society*, *Applied Economics* and the *International Journal of Management Reviews*.

Professor Urwin has a particular focus on the issues faced by government policymakers. Within the UK he has worked with HM Revenue and Customs; the Department for Business, Innovation and Skills; the Ministry of Defence; the Department for Work and Pensions; and the Ministry of Justice. In his work he has collaborated with staff from the Institute for Fiscal Studies, the Centre for Economic Performance at the LSE, the Policy Studies Institute, Cranfield School of Management and Southampton University.

He has supervised PhD and MPhil candidates to successful completion and has acted as a referee for the Economic and Social Research Council and academic journals, including the *Manchester School*, the *Journal of Regional Studies*, the *Southern Economic Journal* and the *Economics of Education Review*.

FOREWORD

In a free economy it is likely that many forms of contractual relationship would develop between somebody who wished to provide services for a business and the business itself. The two most obvious forms of relationship are employment and self-employment. In the former the business has much more control – it is a 'contract of service' – and, in return, the employee has certain benefits and reduced risk. With self-employment, an individual provides certain services to businesses and is remunerated without any guarantee of a continuing relationship.

If economies were undistorted by regulation, we would expect to see the most efficient form of contractual relationships being used in a particular circumstance. Businesses and those who provide services would balance the advantages and disadvantages of taking on employees and contracting with the self-employed. Unfortunately, it is highly likely that government regulation does shape the economy and distorts people's decisions in undesirable ways.

Self-employment is made more attractive as a result of the cost of regulation. This arises especially, though not only, from employment protection regulation. Ironically, if self-employment replaces employment for this reason, then people providing services to businesses will be less secure than if they had employee relationships in unregulated markets. Regulation particularly affects small firms as it is often a fixed cost. This means that there can be a 'hollowing out' of the labour market: more people are self-employed (who would rather not be); at the same time, fewer of the self-employed take on employees and so there are relatively fewer employees working for small businesses. The average size of businesses with employees then rises.

According to Peter Urwin, author of this IEA monograph, this is precisely what is happening. Urwin's research also demonstrates how the social profile of those who are self-employed and those who work for smaller companies is quite different from that of those who work for larger companies. For example, women, individuals from certain ethnic groups, those with young dependants, those with low or no qualifications, those for whom English is not a first language and those who have recently experienced unemployment make up a much greater proportion of the workforce of small firms. If we damage employment in small businesses, we undermine opportunities for those who want flexible working arrangements and for those who find it difficult to persuade larger, more bureaucratic employers of their talents.

Other interesting findings from Urwin's research relate to the nature of entrepreneurship. Only a tiny proportion of today's small firms become tomorrow's large firms. More importantly, the nature of entrepreneurial discovery is such that we cannot predict those firms that will flourish in this way in advance. As such, any policy that involves picking winners or encouraging particular sectors is doomed to failure. Instead, it is important to remove general impediments to the self-employed taking on employees and to small firms growing. This also points in the direction of radical deregulation.

This research monograph is interesting not only because of

its economic evidence and policy conclusions relating to employment regulation. It provides a fascinating insight into the social profile of the self-employed and those who work for small firms. Regulation to improve job security is always tempting for politicians. The costs of this regulation, however, are difficult for politicians to identify – they are reflected in the wealth creation opportunities that are lost and in reduced opportunities for many people with non-standard backgrounds and qualifications who do not fare well in the highly structured labour markets that are the recruiting ground for large firms.

PHILIP BOOTH

Editorial and Programme Director, Institute of Economic Affairs
Professor of Insurance and Risk Management, Cass Business School,
City University
August 2011

The views expressed in this monograph are, as in all IEA publications, those of the authors and not those of the Institute (which has no corporate view), its managing trustees, Academic Advisory Council Members or senior staff.

SUMMARY

- Self-employment is a form of contractual relationship which, in certain circumstances, will have greater benefits to the parties involved than an employer–employee relationship. Government intervention, however, may make self-employment artificially more attractive by raising the costs of employment relationships.
- Certain ethnic minority groups, older people and those without English as a first language tend to be over-represented among the self-employed. This is partly because of the flexibility the arrangement provides but also because self-employment offers a 'safety valve' for those who find it difficult to find employment in the formal labour market.
- It is vital that businesses are not impeded from moving from a situation where the owner is self-employed without employees to a situation where the business has employees. There is evidence that businesses are impeded in this way. In just nine years to 2009, the proportion of micro-businesses with employees fell by almost one fifth. At the same time the proportion of self-employed with no employees rose rapidly.
- Women, individuals from certain ethnic groups, those with young dependants, those with low or no qualifications, those for whom English is not a first language and those who have recently experienced unemployment make up a much greater

proportion of the workforce of small firms. For example, whereas 11 per cent of employees of small firms had no qualifications, only 4 per cent of employees of large firms had no qualifications.

- Some workers will prefer to work for small firms because of the greater flexibility they offer in their working practices. In many cases, however, small firms will employ people who are talented but who are not able to negotiate the more formal recruitment processes of larger firms. Micro-businesses therefore perform an important economic and social function – employing people who might be overlooked by larger employers.
- Genuine entrepreneurial insight and discovery tends to come from small firms. Entrepreneurship is crucial for economic growth. The nature of entrepreneurial insight is such, however, that we have no idea where it will come from – not even in the most general terms. Probably only one in every thousand 'start-up' firms will become one of the large businesses of the future.
- Policies to promote entrepreneurship must come in the form of removing impediments to business and should not involve the promotion of particular business activities. It is simply not possible for government intervention to pick this tiny number of winners. All government can do is create a climate in which entrepreneurship can thrive.
- The smallest firms are a key driver of job creation. Businesses do not start big. One quarter of employees working in firms that were established ten years earlier are working for firms that started from a position of employing only one person.
- The cost of regulation has grown enormously over the

last fifteen years. This particularly affects small firms with employees because regulatory costs act like a 'poll tax'. Wide-ranging exemptions from employment regulation and the minimum wage would be appropriate for small firms. Such exemptions would have the additional advantage of allowing the government to 'experiment' with deregulation. Standard terms and conditions of employment could be drawn up which would ensure that employees clearly understood the exemptions. Radical reforms of the tax system would also assist small firms which experience much greater compliance costs than large firms.

- Moves by the government to promote entrepreneurship through the state education system or provide specific tax exemptions and reliefs for particular forms of business activity are wasteful or counterproductive.

ACKNOWLEDGEMENTS

This publication has been made possible by the Nigel Vinson Charitable Foundation. The directors and trustees of the IEA thank the Rt Hon. Lord Vinson of Roddam Dene, LVO, for both his intellectual and financial input.

Many thanks to J. R. Shackleton, Giorgio Di Pietro, Franz Buscha, Abby Ghobadian, Alan Urwin, John Spindler and anonymous referees for helpful comments.

This report uses data from the 2004 *Workplace Employment Relations Series* (WERS) and the 1994, 1997, 2002, 2007 and 2009 quarterly *Labour Force Surveys* (LFS). The LFS is distributed by the Economic and Social Data Service; Crown Copyright material is reproduced with the permission of the Controller of HMSO and the Queen's Printer for Scotland. The WERS is jointly sponsored by the Department for Business, Innovation and Skills; the Economic and Social Research Council (ESRC); the Advisory, Conciliation and Arbitration Service (Acas); and the Policy Studies Institute (PSI).

ABBREVIATIONS AND ACRONYMS

BIS   Department for Business, Innovation and Skills
CIPD   Chartered Institute for Personnel and Development
DDA   Disability Discrimination Act
DWP   Department for Work and Pensions
EPL   Employment protection legislation
FSB   Federation of Small Businesses
HGF   High-growth firm
HMRC   HM Revenue and Customs
HSE   Health and Safety Executive
ILO   International Labour Organisation
LFS   *Labour Force Survey*
NICs   National Insurance contributions
OECD   Organisation for Economic Co-operation and Development
PMR   Product Market Regulation
R&D   Research and development
SME   Small to medium-sized enterprises
WERS   *Workplace Employment Relations Survey*

TABLES AND FIGURES

AUTHOR'S PREFACE

Among citizens of the EU, evidence suggests that 45 per cent would prefer self-employment to alternatives if they could choose freely: in the UK this figure is almost identical. The attraction of working for oneself is tempered, however, by the realities of self-employment, which many understand as a much less secure form of working. For example, over half of all new businesses created will not be in existence five years later. As a result, at any point in time only 12 per cent of UK working-age adults are seriously thinking of starting up their own business, and for the last twenty years the proportion of workers who are actually self-employed has hovered at around the same rate.

Even from such a brief description it would seem reasonable to suggest that less risk-averse individuals, who relish the challenge of 'being their own boss', should be left to decide whether self-employment is for them. For those who crave more stability and are willing to submit to a greater degree of control in their working lives, an employee job may be preferable. The self-employed find themselves, however, at the centre of various key policy debates, with suggestions that they are essential to an entrepreneurial society often countered by concerns over employment security and suspicion from the tax authorities. This monograph considers a wealth of evidence on various aspects of self-employment and draws this together to make suggestions for policy.

The status quo does not represent a situation where individuals and firms are taking decisions based purely on the untainted risks and rewards of self-employment relative to alternatives. The structure of the UK tax system produces incentives for employers and workers to declare employment relationships as being between a firm and a self-employed individual (as opposed to an employee). But we might ask whether this distortion of incentives is really such a bad thing, given the perceived importance among many commentators of the role that entrepreneurship plays in the economy. The tax system can be seen as one of many government-sponsored inducements to promote entrepreneurship. Unfortunately, however, evidence suggests that much of the regulation and legislation produced by government acts as a barrier to growth for self-employed small business owners. The activities of government may be simultaneously creating incentives for individuals to become self-employed, but then erecting barriers to the growth of the firms they would create.

Chapter 2 considers the behaviour of firms and individuals in determining the levels of self-employment, and how the various regulatory pressures 'net out'. In doing so, we take a first step towards a clearer understanding of what drives self-employment and begin to distinguish between the self-employed with, and those without, employees – something that is essential in understanding the social and economic contributions of the self-employed.

Chapter 3 introduces a literature on self-employment which debates whether individuals are 'pushed out' of employment or 'pulled in' to self-employment. The push–pull debate has typically arisen as a comment on the higher levels of self-employment often seen among groups that face disadvantage in the labour market.

For instance, some ethnic minority groups have particularly pronounced levels of self-employment – something that could result from the entrepreneurial spirit that is often seen among immigrant communities (pulling them into self-employment), or from a lack of employee job opportunities as a result of discrimination or other labour market disadvantages (something that may be seen as pushing them into self-employment). This debate hints at a potential role for self-employment as a 'safety valve' for those who cannot supply their skills to the market because of barriers they face in becoming an employee. An analysis of data from the 2009 *Labour Force Survey* (LFS) considers rates of self-employment among groups in society who may face disadvantage, such as the unemployed and those experiencing language difficulties. In the second half of the chapter we further develop this analysis of LFS data by considering the job opportunities that self-employed small business owners create. The suggestion is that the self-employed also seem to create employment opportunities that are more likely to be filled by individuals from disadvantaged groups.

Highlighting these differences in the 'nature' or 'mix' of employment opportunities created by smaller businesses moves us towards a focus on the self-employed with employees. Chapter 4 considers the contribution that small businesses make to overall job creation: research in this area would seem to underline the importance of new business 'start-ups', which continually create and destroy a large number of jobs. Recently commissioned work in the UK, however, has tended to focus on identifying the 'high-growth' firms that rise from this start-up ferment. These two approaches provide an excellent backdrop to a policy debate over whether the continual creation and destruction of jobs by start-ups has a value in itself, separate and distinct from any 'net' positions.

While the empirical evidence on job creation and destruction is quite extensive, it still does not allow us enough insight into the Schumpeterian process of creative destruction to provide clear policy guidance. Having exhausted empirics, Chapter 5 draws on various strands of economic theory to construct a picture of this process of creative destruction and how it relates to theories of firm creation and self-employment. At the centre of this discussion is the entrepreneur. The main aim of this chapter is to clarify what we mean by this term, how entrepreneurial insight feeds into the economy and whether or not self-employment plays an important role in this.

The monograph begins with an introduction which sets the scene for our discussions. The final chapter concludes with a discussion of the main findings and considers possible policy prescriptions for the wider economy. Chapter 6 suggests what could be done to better align incentives in light of our findings.

1 SELF-EMPLOYMENT IN THE UK

Developments in working arrangements that led to the modern-day distinction between 'employees' and the 'self-employed' can be traced back to the advent of industrial relations at the start of the twentieth century.[1] Before this, in the early years of the Industrial Revolution, those supplying labour (as opposed to capitalists and landowners) were essentially self-employed. They had few of the benefits and security of contract that we associate with modern employees. Similarly, while employers held the balance of power in these years before widespread unionisation, workers did not systematically provide, for instance, fixed periods of notice. This relationship between business owners and workers was essentially the same as that which had prevailed for itinerant workers since antiquity.

As the economy of the UK and other countries industrialised, employers needed to exert greater control over large numbers of workers to coordinate their business activity. They therefore sought contracts of employment that imposed a wider subordination[2] and, in return, groups of workers organised to secure

---

1 While Roman Law did allow some distinction between the promise to deliver a certain quantity of labour (*locatio conductio operarum*) as opposed to a defined product or service (*locatio conductio operis*), this is more a distinction between 'piece rate' (payment by results or output) and payment for (labour) input.

2 In the words of Sir Otto Kahn-Freund, the employee contract, 'in its inception ... is an act of submission' and 'in its operation it is a condition of subordination'.

holiday pay, sick leave and a greater level of employment protection. These increasingly complicated agreements required more advanced legal infrastructure, especially when compared with the relative simplicity of arrangements between the self-employed and those commissioning work. As Freedman (2001) details, the development of an employee/self-employed distinction has been through case law, rather than any statutory definition of these terms.

When we consider the modern world, economies at an earlier stage of development tend to have much higher proportions of self-employed workers (see, for instance, Blanchflower, 2004)[3] and most countries of the OECD have witnessed a systematic decline in the proportion of self-employed workers over the last half-century. Other than this long-term decline which tends to accompany industrialisation, however, the experiences of developed nations are far from uniform. According to figures from the OECD (reproduced in Parker, 2004), between 1960 and 2000 the rate of (non-agricultural) self-employment in the USA fell from 10.5 per cent to 6.5 per cent; in Canada it remained relatively stable (moving from 10 per cent to 9.5 per cent), while in France it fell from 17 per cent to 8 per cent.

There would seem to be many different factors at work here, but the UK does stand out in some respects. The rate of UK self-employment started from a comparatively low base of 6 per cent in 1960; it then increased to a level (11 per cent) in 2000 that was closer to the OECD average and is now around 13 per cent (LFS, 2009)[4] – a rate that is relatively high when compared with

---

3   Parker (2004) argues along the same lines, citing the lack of 'infrastructure' in less developed economies.

4   According to the UK *Labour Force Survey*, in the period April to June 2009 the

countries at a similar stage of development (ibid.). This figure as a proportion of employees may still not seem high, but a breakdown of this overall percentage in Table 1 underlines how important a form of working it is for women and men of certain ages.

Table 1 **Gender and age of employees and the self-employed in the UK**

	Age groups					
	16–24	25–39	40–49	50–64	65+	Total
Male						
Employee	1,811,076	4,443,460	3,113,242	3,006,300	246,188	12,620,266
	94.13%	85.46%	80.29%	76.93%	58.12%	82.31%
Self-employed	112,853	756,257	764,491	901,597	177,398	2,712,596
	5.87%	14.54%	19.71%	23.07%	41.88%	17.69%
Male total	1,923,929	5,199,717	3,877,733	3,907,897	423,586	15,332,862
Female						
Employee	1,773,306	4,099,119	3,196,598	2,965,685	218,890	12,253,598
	97.97%	92.88%	90.26%	90.20%	77.45%	91.89%
Self-employed	36,675	314,085	344,992	322,180	63,723	1,081,655
	2.03%	7.12%	9.74%	9.80%	22.55%	8.11%
Female total	1,809,981	4,413,204	3,541,590	3,287,865	282,613	13,335,253

Source: Quarterly *Labour Force Survey*, April–June 2009
For ease of exposition, Table 1 does not include those on government training programmes and unpaid family workers who make up around 0.7 per cent of those in employment.

Table 1 underlines the gender difference in rates of self-employment across the UK. The self-employment rate is close to one in five for employed men of all ages (18 per cent), compared with only 8 per cent of women. For men in the later stages of their

number of workers who categorised themselves as being self-employed stood at 3.6 million, or 12.7 per cent of those in employment.

career self-employment becomes even more important, with close to one quarter of 50- to 64-year-olds adopting this form of working. For women of all ages below 65, on the other hand, we do not observe self-employment rates higher than 10 per cent. For both men and women aged 65 and above, however, rates of self-employment are approximately double those seen in younger age groups.

The possible reasons why self-employment is particularly pronounced among those aged 65 and above can be seen as characteristic of the wider debate on the pros and cons of being an employee, when compared with self-employment. For many years there have been predictions that individuals in the UK will need to continue working beyond current accepted retirement ages, if the public and private finances are to cope with ageing populations (Urwin, 2006). Before the 2011 removal of a firm's right to set a default retirement age, however, many workers did not have the option of a 'phased' retirement (with fewer working hours and responsibilities) with their present employer (Urwin et al., 2011). In this context, Table 1 could be taken as evidence that self-employment facilitates working into old age, as it allows greater independence and control over working hours and can therefore be seen as more flexible.

But the flexibility associated with working for oneself, which derives from the control over working arrangements, also entails greater responsibility and an increase in risk. In Table 1, higher rates of self-employment after the age of retirement could also be a result of older workers taking on a riskier form of employment because of a lack of opportunities to be an employee, coupled with insufficient savings for retirement. This trade-off is at the heart of many economic models that adopt a risk-adjusted approach to the consideration of whether individuals choose self-employment over other forms of working (see, for instance, Rees and Shah, 1986).

In this particular example 62 per cent of the self-employed men and women aged 65 and above in Table 1 are 'Managers, Professionals or Associate professionals' (LFS, 2009) – a group of individuals who face greater choice as to whether or not they work into old age (ibid.). The pensions crisis has hit all levels of society, however, and evidence suggests the self-employed are particularly more likely to work into old age[5] – it may be that this group has a greater opportunity to work into old age, but necessity is what drives them. This issue of choice versus necessity has been posed as a question of whether individuals are 'pushed out or pulled in' (see, for instance, Clark and Drinkwater, 2000). That is, are the self-employed pulled into self-employment because of, for instance, the attraction of being their own boss or are they pushed to consider this form of working as a consequence of fewer employee job opportunities (i.e. being 'pushed out' of other parts of the labour market)?

As one might expect, the findings from research studies describe a more nuanced picture as choice is always bounded. We can already see that working as a self-employed person has pros and cons very different from the arrangements that exist for employees. The question of who becomes self-employed, and why, is a central focus of Chapter 2, and Chapter 3 considers how this relates to the discernible differences in characteristics between the self-employed and employees. In all of this, the *Labour Force Survey* (LFS) is the main source of information.[6] This study also draws on

5   As we shall discuss later, the self-employed with employees are often recorded as being managers, rather than under the occupation associated with their firm.

6   The LFS is designed to contact approximately 1 household in every 500 – around

other sources of data, however, and, in order to ensure consistency, we need to define self-employment. Unfortunately this is not a straightforward task, and consideration of the reasons why provides essential insights into one of the key policy debates on the value of self-employment.

What is self-employment?

At first glance it seems pretty straightforward to characterise the difference between those who are self-employed and those working as employees. In the case of the self-employed we should observe a *contract for services* (where one party agrees to pay a certain price for the delivery of specified goods or services), as opposed to the *contract of service*, which typifies the modern-day employer–employee relationship (involving a wider subordination and agreement to take orders, in exchange for greater security and other benefits). The guidance given by HM Revenue and Customs (HMRC), however, which is a key determinant of how working relationships are considered, underlines that things are much less straightforward in reality. The following is reproduced from the direction given by HMRC on whether an individual is employed or self-employed.

There is clearly a legal grey area somewhere between being an employee and self-employed, with recent legal cases failing to clarify the situation. A High Court ruling in July 2008 (*Minister for Agriculture and Food* v. *Barry*), which provided detailed analysis

80,000 UK households – and to collect data on all adult members of each sampled household. It was carried out biennially between 1973 and 1983, annually between 1984 and 1991 and quarterly from the spring of 1992, and provides extensive information on those who report themselves as being either self-employed or an employee.

Contract of service, for services and the self-employed

For tax and NICs purposes, there is no statutory definition of a contract of service or of a contract for services. What the parties call their relationship, or what they consider it to be, is not conclusive. It is the reality of the relationship which matters.

In order to determine the nature of a contract, it is necessary to apply common law principles. The courts have, over the years, laid down some factors and tests that are relevant, which are included in the overview below.

If the answer is 'Yes' to all of the following questions, then the worker is probably an employee:

- Do they have to do the work themselves?
- Can someone tell them at any time what to do, where to carry out the work or when and how to do it?
- Can they work a set amount of hours?
- Can someone move them from task to task?
- Are they paid by the hour, week, or month?
- Can they get overtime pay or bonus payment?

If the answer is 'Yes' to all of the following questions, it will usually mean that the worker is self-employed:

- Can they hire someone to do the work or engage helpers at their own expense?
- Do they risk their own money?
- Do they provide the main items of equipment they need to do their job, not just the small tools that many employees provide for themselves?
- Do they agree to do a job for a fixed price regardless of how long the job may take?
- Can they decide what work to do, how and when to do the work and where to provide the services?
- Do they regularly work for a number of different people?
- Do they have to correct unsatisfactory work in their own time and at their own expense?

Source: http://www.hmrc.gov.uk/employment-status/index.htm

of the jurisprudence on the tests outlined in the box, only served to underline the difficulties in this area.[7] The reason that this is so hotly debated is that, for any given set of activities, the employer–employee relationship provides greater revenue to the UK tax authorities. There is an incentive for employers and employees to define working relationships as contract for service and for HMRC to ensure that this is not simply a way of avoiding tax.

Returning to our consideration of the LFS, technical guidance[8] suggests that those who are recorded as self-employed in the LFS are supposed to be meeting the criteria set out in the box. While the same parameters are being used in distinguishing those who are working under contract *for*, rather than *of*, service, the individual respondent ultimately decides in the LFS whether they should be categorised as self-employed. In contrast, individuals wishing to register for tax purposes will find that there is no 'self-employed' category. Rather the self-employed have options, which include the setting up of companies, partnerships and sole proprietorships. As a result of this, when drawing on business surveys (as opposed to household surveys such as the LFS) we are presented with a differing set of figures.

Consider evidence from the Enterprise Directorate Analytical Unit at BIS, which takes as its starting point a business-based register (the Inter Departmental Business Register, IDBR[9]) and then supplements this with information from the LFS. Figure

---

7   For more details, see comment by the International Law Office at http://www.internationallawoffice.com/newsletters/detail.aspx?g=b9703708-18a9-44a2-a2a7-d4691c940bac.

8   *Labour Force Survey User Guide*, vol. 5: *LFS Classifications*, 2009, pp. 21–2.

9   Which deals mainly with firms that are VAT registered – in 2008/09 firms had to be be VAT registered when taxable turnover rose above £67,000 per annum (though short-term exemptions could be requested).

1 uses these BIS data to track changes in the proportions of different-sized firms in the UK economy (as measured by the number of employees) between 1997 and 2009. For instance, the final column reflects BIS estimates that in 2009 there were just over 3.6 million enterprises with no employees; just over one million 'micro' enterprises employing between one and nine employees; just under 170,000 businesses employing between 10 and 49 employees; and approximately 36,000 businesses among the remaining medium-sized and large enterprises.[10]

Comparing these data with the data for self-employed without employees from the LFS, the BIS estimates seem at first to be a little high. The April–June 2009 LFS suggests there were just under 3.8 million respondents classified as self-employed and, of these, just under three million reported not having employees. The BIS figures, however, will also include enterprises being run by the 400,000 who report in the LFS that they have a second job as a self-employed individual – in other words, it is possible for somebody to be both self-employed and also employed by another organisation. In addition, from 2000 we see a jump in the BIS figures for self-employed with no employees, and this is due to the inclusion of single-employee companies in the zero-employees category.[11] When considering LFS statistics later in this text we need to keep these differences in mind.[12]

---

10 Strictly speaking, small to medium-sized enterprises (SMEs) have fewer than 250 employees; and within this category, firms with one to 49 employees are 'small', while 'micro' enterprises employ fewer than ten employees.

11 To better reflect the fact that many single-employee firms were actually those where the sole proprietor was also being paid as an employee.

12 For a more detailed discussion, see BERR, *Small and Medium-sized Enterprises (SME) Statistics for the UK; Methodology and Accuracy Technical Note*, Enterprise Directorate, 2006.

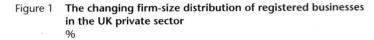

Figure 1   **The changing firm-size distribution of registered businesses
in the UK private sector**
%

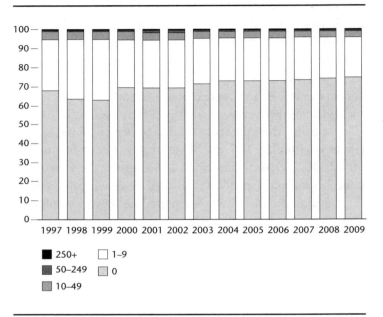

The aim here is not to get into a technical discussion of the
pros and cons of different datasets, but simply to underline the
fact that legally, empirically and, as we shall see later, theoreti-
cally, it is hard to find one consistent definition of what it is to
be self-employed. The technical notes accompanying the BIS data
make the point very well when they suggest 'there is no lower
boundary for inclusion in the SME Statistics', and the smallest
amounts of 'enterprise activity' count. More specifically, the
category of self-employed without employees is likely to contain

'labour-only sub-contractors ... [possibly] work[ing] for just one customer', as well as 'genuine entrepreneurs ... separate from the organisation to which they sell their skills', and those whose 'employers have simply shifted their job from employee to self-employed status'.[13]

Self-employment without employees grows while the smallest businesses are squeezed out

Whether we consider the LFS or BIS estimates, there is one common story. Even if we discount the increase in the zero-employees category in 2000 which results from a change in statistical practice, there remains an apparent 'squeezing' of the proportion of micro-business (with one to nine employees) from 2000 onwards in Figure 1. The proportion of firms without employees grows from 69.6 per cent of all firms in 2000 to 74.8 per cent in 2009. At the same time there is a fall in the proportion of micro-businesses with employees from 25.4 to 21.0 per cent. These changes in the proportion of businesses of different sizes are set against a backdrop of expanding numbers of total enterprises.

This fall in the proportion of micro-enterprises with employees has not been accompanied by a significant fall in the proportion of people working for micro-enterprises. The proportion of the workforce employed by larger firms has fallen, however. Businesses with 250+ employees saw their share of total employment fall from 44.9 per cent to 40.3 per cent between 2000 and 2009, while all other firms with any employees retained a

13   Enterprise Directorate, *Small and Medium-sized Enterprise (SME) Statistics for the UK and Regions: Methodology Note*, BIS, 2009, p. 6.

similar proportion of employment over the period. The falling proportion of employees in the largest firms was countered by a rising proportion of employment accounted for by enterprises with no employees (the self-employed without employees) from 13.5 to 17.3 per cent over the period.

Thus we have a rising number of self-employed individuals with no employees; a likely rise in the average size of micro-enterprises employing between one and nine employees; and a fall in the proportionate importance of the largest firms. In light of our later discussions on the impacts of regulation and legislation, these may be seen as worrying developments. It is the increase in the proportion of employment accounted for by the self-employed without employees, however, which has been the focus of most attention, as it continues a trend that can be traced back to the 1980s. Between 1981 and 1991 the proportion of self-employed without employees increased from 61 per cent to 69 per cent of all self-employed (Campbell and Daly, 1992: 269). Figures from the April–June quarters of the LFS suggest that by 1996 this figure had risen to 74 per cent, and by 2009 79 per cent of the self-employed reported that they had no employees. These changes tend to be set against rising overall numbers of self-employed: for instance, between 1996 and 2009 there was an increase of 420,000 in the number of self-employed without employees, compared with an increase of only 110,000 with employees (LFS, 1996 and 2009, April–June quarters).

The fact that growth in self-employment has been due mainly to those without employees continues to fuel concerns that motivations have more to do with the incentives in the tax system. In addition, towards the end of the recent boom an increasing proportion of all new job creation was attributed to increases in self-employment (Lindsay and Macaulay, 2004; Blanchflower, 2007). For instance, of the estimated 305,000 jobs created between quarter one 2005 and quarter one 2007, an estimated 217,000 were attributed to an increase in self-employment (ibid.). The reasons for such trends have been variously attributed to the influx of eastern European workers (who are concentrated in sectors such as construction, where self-employment is extensive) as well as increased housing equity and lower interest rates, which ease access to finance for start-ups.

In the following chapters, when we return to these debates, evidence from the LFS is considered on both the self-employed (with and without employees) and small businesses. In all of this analysis the underlying assumption is that the self-employed with employees predominate among micro-businesses and then, as we move up through small and into medium-sized firms, enterprises are less and less likely to be run by self-employed owner-managers. Analysing the largest category of businesses, we are unlikely to be considering any enterprises run by the self-employed.

Self-employment and entrepreneurship

Similarly, there is no distinction made here between self-employment and entrepreneurship. We are thereby initially following the direction of a number of commentators, who use the terms interchangeably even when there is a recognised need for some distinction (Blanchflower and Oswald, 1998; Blanchflower, 2000, 2004). As we delve deeper into the issues of self-employment, however, it becomes clear that entrepreneurship is distinct from self-employment. Chapter 5 draws on various strands of economic theory to clarify this distinction and weigh the validity of competing arguments over the role and value that self-employment plays in supplying entrepreneurial insight to the economy.

It may seem strange that we need to clarify the economic value that the self-employed and small businesses bring to the economy. As we have seen, the suggestion is that small and medium-sized enterprises (SMEs) account for 60 per cent of all private sector employment and 49 per cent of all private sector turnover (ibid.). Our discussions also suggest, however, that a rise in new business generation, which could be hailed as indicative of an increasing entrepreneurial spirit, could also be a result of firms and individuals moving towards a focus on short-term consultancy arrangements simply because of the tax advantages. In this, we are weighing the evidence that there is some potential for a worsening of employment conditions in outsourcing scenarios (see, for instance, Georgellis and Wall, 2000; Clark et al., 1998) against the potential benefits to employment generation of small firms (detailed originally by Birch, 1979, 1981, 1987) and the creative destruction of Schumpeter (1934, 1937).

2 WHY DO PEOPLE CHOOSE SELF-EMPLOYMENT?

This chapter considers the motivations for taking up self-employment and subcontracting as a form of working arrangement. From these discussions we are able to speculate on the discernible differences in characteristics that might be expected between the self-employed and employees. The chapter begins by identifying a high propensity to become self-employed across the population of the UK and suggests why a focus on entrepreneurship (as opposed to self-employment) across government departments may often hinder serious policy debate. We then consider why we may expect to observe certain types of individual in self-employment. Evidence on the incentives produced by the interaction of the tax and regulatory environments is then discussed before a consideration of the issues around access to finance for those wishing to set up their own business. Finally, the chapter concludes with the results of statistical analysis designed to identify those factors most closely associated with an individual being observed as self-employed as opposed to being an employee.

Alan Sugar and the disgruntled dreamers

The Small Business Service (SBS) *Household Survey of Entrepreneurship 2007* suggests that the proportion of individuals thinking of starting up on their own stayed roughly constant in the UK at between 11 and 12 per cent from 2001 to 2007;[1] this is close to the proportion actually observed in self-employment. While these figures are not directly comparable with those produced as part of the Global Entrepreneurship Monitor (GEM) (Bosma and Levie, 2009), the latter suggests that the proportion with 'entrepreneurial intentions' among the working-age population of the UK is not particularly high when compared with other countries at a similar stage of development.

In the GEM figures, however, the USA ranks alongside Switzerland in terms of the proportion of the population thinking of starting up on their own (and both rank above the UK). As our discussions in the previous chapter (and those of the GEM researchers) underline, there is a lot that is likely to influence, and be influenced by, the levels of entrepreneurship in an economy. It is interesting to note, however, that we have suddenly moved from the use of 'self-employment' as our moniker to 'entrepreneurship'. As suggested in later chapters, the two terms are distinct, but in the discussions here we are essentially still considering self-employment.

Unfortunately 'global self-employment monitor' does not have quite the same ring and the 'household study of self-employment' might not have received such generous funding from government. This is where we come to our first potential concern for UK policymakers. Entrepreneurship is actively promoted by government and new surveys are funded to provide detailed investigation over many years. In contrast, the self-employed (particularly those without employees) do not seem to achieve the same level of

1   IFF Research, *BERR Household Survey of Entrepreneurship 2007*, Research report prepared for the Department for Business, Enterprise and Regulatory Reform (BERR), 2008.

specific policy focus (see the previous discussion on the potential for investigation by HMRC) – a situation that is in stark contrast to the explicit promotion and support of self-employment during the 1980s.[2] For instance, one of the nine Structural Reform Priorities of the Department for Business, Innovation and Skills (BIS) 2011–2015 Business Plan is to 'Boost enterprise and make this the decade of the entrepreneur'[3] (p. 3). While this publication mentions promoting entrepreneurship and supporting small businesses extensively, it makes no specific reference to self-employment.

This may be a case of policymakers wishing to derive kudos from the use of more dynamic terminology, but in doing so it may suppress serious policy debate. Very few people are going to argue against the promotion of 'entrepreneurship', but unfortunately in using such terminology we divert attention from important policy questions relating to the way that government perceives self-employment. Entrepreneurship is seen as such a universally good thing that very few people ask the question (i) whether it is possible and/or desirable to increase the levels of entrepreneurship in the economy (though see Baumol, 1990) and, if the answer is yes, (ii) if this is a role best carried out by government.

For instance, it is quite possible that increasing the number of start-ups will simply increase the number of business failures. This is a question to which we return in detail in Chapter 4. But even if levels of entrepreneurship can be usefully boosted, many commentators have pointed out that reality TV is more likely to have had an effect on people's views than government policy

2   See, for instance, Fraser and Greene (2004) for a detailed discussion.

3   http://www.bis.gov.uk/assets/biscore/corporate/docs/b/10-p58-bis-business-plan.pdf.

(see Blanchflower, 2007). As one commentator from the USA has suggested: 'When I was in college, guys usually pretended they were in a band, now they pretend they are in a start-up' (Economist, 2009) – making certain activities 'cool' is not a core competence that one associates with politicians, civil servants and academics.

It would seem reasonable to suggest that entrepreneurship needs to be lauded to be taken seriously by those with talent. At a house party in the UK, would an individual be seen in a positive light if they announced that they had started their own business, as opposed to securing an employee position in one of the blue-chip firms? If we believe that such a change in attitudes has taken place, it is unlikely to be a result of government targets, whereas unfortunately reality TV and Hollywood blockbusters may have infused some glamour into the 'business start-up'. In a comment on government policy, David Landes suggests that 'You can build as many incubators as you like, but if only 3 per cent of the population want to be entrepreneurs ... you will have trouble creating an entrepreneurial economy' (ibid.).

More importantly in providing value for money in the use of public funds, we need to consider carefully what value surveys of entrepreneurial intention bring to our deliberations. As a study by Henley (2007) suggests, 'the majority of transitions [into self-employment] are not preceded by a statement of aspiration a year earlier'. While the author emphasises the lack of preparedness among many new ventures that this suggests, it also calls into question the value of surveys that collect information on entre-preneurial intention. There are further questions raised over the insights that 'intention' can provide, when studies suggest that 46 per cent of the UK population would, if they could, choose

Why start up on your own?
a) the freedom to adopt one's own approach to work;
b) to challenge oneself;
c) to make more money;
d) to be one's own boss;
e) to make an idea or innovation happen;
f) to fill a gap in the market.

Source: SBS *Household Survey of Entrepreneurship*

to be self-employed (Gallup Organisation, 2010). It is perhaps because of consideration of the above main reasons reported by individuals intending to start up their own firm (Small Business Service, 2007), however, that we see the weakness of such surveys in providing insight that is of use to policymakers.

All of the desires from a) to d) could potentially apply to a large swathe of the UK adult population, whether self-employed or working as an employee, and only e) and f) would seem to move us towards some concept of entrepreneurship. The motivations of those who report a desire to become self-employed provide little insight into the reasons why people become self-employed. If we questioned a sample of individuals who had chosen employee jobs, a large proportion would likely report some desire to 'make more money', 'challenge themselves' and 'be their own boss' (implying search for a more autonomous employee job). Similarly, questions must be asked as to the value of international comparisons of entrepreneurial intention, when the USA has levels similar to those in Switzerland.

From desire to decision: who becomes self-employed?

As in the UK, many individuals in OECD countries report a desire to become self-employed, but relatively few actually do so (Burke et al., 2000, 2002; Blanchflower et al., 2001; Constant et al., 2007).

This section attempts to present a more objective picture of the differences between those who turn a desire to be their own boss into reality and those who decide to become employees.

Sector and occupation

As a first step in developing a picture of the drivers of self-employment, Table 2 provides an overview of the sector and occupational concentrations of self-employment in the UK in 2009. Each cell in the table contains a figure for the proportion of workers within a particular occupation and industry grouping who report themselves as self-employed. Some outliers stand out. For instance, there are 1.16 million in the *Skilled Trades* working within the *Construction* sector and 638,000 of these (55 per cent) are self-employed according to weighted figures from the LFS.

It would appear that the differing nature of products and services across sectors of the economy has the potential to have an impact on working arrangements. Indeed, there is a history of considering specific sectors as case studies because they have characteristics that seem particularly associated with higher levels of self-employment: the study by Granger et al. (1995) of the book-publishing industry is a case in point. Similarly, the exact nature and timing of each worker's contribution to the production and delivery processes (proxied by occupation) may have an impact in a way that leads to more or less of a predominance of self-employment. For instance, other things remaining equal, sectors that experience more volatile and unpredictable demand conditions, or where occupational inputs are required only infrequently (for projects with a specific timeline), are more likely to be characterised by outsourcing relationships as a way of managing risk.

It is clear from Table 2 that there are quite substantial variations in the proportions of workers in sector-occupation groups. There are, however, some artefacts of the data. For example, the apparent concentration of self-employment among *Managers and Senior Officials*, and the corresponding low concentration among *Admin. & Secretarial/Sales and Customer Services*, arises because somebody who is self-employed and runs a marketing firm would be counted as a manager rather than as somebody who is in a sales and customer service occupation. Other than this, *Other Services* (which includes dry-cleaners, hairdressers, etc.), *Professional, Scientific and Technical* activities (which spans R&D, accountancy, and legal and technical activities) and the *Construction* sector all have particularly pronounced levels of self-employment across a number of different occupations.

As we shall see in our following discussions of regulation and legislation, the high levels of self-employment in *Construction* are associated with particular policies towards self-employed persons in this sector (see, for instance, Harvey and Behling, 2010). This has raised particular concern among the UK tax authorities, and there is ongoing debate over the extent to which this is 'false self-employment'[4] – i.e. reporting for tax purposes people who are self-employed but in reality working under arrangements that one would expect of an employee.

From Table 2, however, one can see two sides to this

---

4   HM Treasury/HM Revenue & Customs, *False self-employment in construction: taxation of workers –summary of consultation responses*, March 2010, para 1.5.

Table 2 **The concentration of self-employment by sector and occupation in the UK**

Main job	Managers and senior officials	Professional occupations	Assoc. professionals and technical	Admin. and secretarial
Manufacturing	9%	5%	6%	2%
Electricity, gas and water supply	4%	8%	1%	1%
Construction	20%	16%	10%	7%
Wholesale, retail, repair of vehicles	23%	23%	13%	2%
Transport and storage	10%	2%	8%	3%
Accommodation and food services	32%	23%	8%	3%
Information and communication	10%	17%	23%	6%
Financial and insurance activities	5%	7%	11%	0%
Real estate activities	25%	14%	19%	10%
Prof., scientific, technical activities	12%	30%	35%	11%
Admin. and support services	17%	9%	12%	6%
Public admin. and defence	1%	5%	1%	0%
Education	11%	6%	18%	2%
Health and social work	4%	19%	6%	1%
Arts, entertainment and recreation	11%	13%	53%	5%
Other service activities	33%	22%	20%	6%
Total occupation percentage	15%	13%	14%	3%
Total frequency	4,480,392	3,911,665	4,233,702	3,273,83

Source: Quarterly *Labour Force Survey*, April–June 2009

ed trades upations	Personal service occupations	Sales and customer service occupations	Process, plant and machine operatives	Elementary occupations	Total sector percentage	Total frequency
3%	14%	5%	2%	2%	6%	2,761,429
0%	0%	3%	5%	5%	4%	151,021
55%	0%	0%	20%	26%	36%	2,378,902
21%	7%	3%	2%	2%	9%	3,979,064
3%	3%	3%	36%	5%	18%	1,496,016
3%	14%	5%	2%	1%	9%	1,355,857
3%	39%	2%	17%	0%	14%	1,007,714
0%	0%	6%	0%	0%	5%	1,232,123
8%	0%	5%	19%	8%	16%	267,115
31%	4%	9%	4%	8%	23%	1,875,521
51%	16%	3%	9%	18%	18%	1,293,730
5%	1%	2%	0%	1%	1%	1,950,323
1%	1%	0%	85%	0%	6%	2,909,740
0%	7%	0%	2%	1%	7%	3,716,339
12%	4%	2%	4%	1%	21%	756,219
38%	38%	6%	19%	23%	28%	751,462
35%	9%	3%	17%	7%	13%	
050,072	2,498,352	2,107,018	1,989,836	3,248,614		28,793,482

argument. Looking across the occupations within the construction sector, there are exceptionally high levels of self-employment among the *Skilled Trades, Process, Plant and Machine* operatives and the *Elementary* occupations; in contrast to the highest three occupations in this sector, which do not have such high self-employment rates. When we look down the columns, however, it is also clear that those in the *Skilled Trades* and *Process, Plant and Machine* categories are more likely to be working as self-employed in quite a few of the sectors under consideration.

As a starting point it would seem reasonable to suggest that, even in the absence of distorting incentives from taxation, regulation and legislation, the industrial (and related occupational) structure of the economy has an impact on the opportunities that individuals face in terms of becoming an employee, as opposed to a self-employed worker. It may be the case that, in the construction sector, the relatively large scale of much work and the up-front fixed costs result in a few firms dominating the sector; but, at the same time, the fixed-term project-based nature of the work favours outsourcing arrangements for many who would otherwise be employees. In contrast, the 'lifestyle' sectors are perhaps less likely to experience economies of scale and there is the potential for product/service differentiation, and therefore one sees a widespread small-business and self-employment culture in this sector too. The explanations may be different in each case but, nevertheless, there are coherent explanations that relate to the economic nature of the activity.

The individual, risks and returns

If you want to become a skilled tradesperson in the construction sector, then your opportunities for gaining an employee job are likely to be limited. But it is still the case that, in any one sector, we observe some individuals from the same occupation working as employees and some as self-employed. What guidance does the existing theoretical and empirical literature give as to why we might observe an individual supplying their labour as a self-employed person rather than as an employee?

Many economic models that capture the individual's process of deciding between self-employment and an employee job have as their starting point the relative financial returns from these two forms of working (Rees and Shah, 1986; Evans and Jovanovic, 1989; Parker, 2004: 26). The modelling approaches then attempt to incorporate liquidity constraints (Kan and Tsai, 2006) or not (de Wit, 1993), as well as a range of additional explanatory variables that describe the situation of the individual (Clark and Drinkwater, 2000). Other theoretical specifications (for instance, Parker, 2004; 24; Blanchflower and Oswald, 1998) define the trade-offs in more general terms by considering the relative utility derived from the two forms of working, thus allowing for non-pecuniary returns. Many of the findings arising from these various models will be considered in later chapters, but for the moment we concentrate on one particular aspect: the role of uncertainty in self-employment and the potential for individuals to consider this form of employment less favourably (Cressy, 2000).

Unfortunately, the *Labour Force Survey* does not collect earnings information from the self-employed. This is partly due to the problems that arise when comparing the financial returns to self-employment with those for employees. Under-reporting is high among the self-employed; they tend to have much lower response rates and part of the earnings of the self-employed is a return to capital. Of the evidence that attempts to overcome these problems, however, the suggestion is that the earnings of the self-employed exhibit much more variability when compared with the wages of employees (Parker et al., 2005) and that earnings inequality is therefore much more pronounced among the self-employed (Meager et al., 1996).

There are questions over the extent to which average (or expected) returns from self-employment are higher or lower than those accruing to employees with similar skills and abilities (see, for instance, Hamilton, 2000). The more pronounced variability in earnings (around this average) for the self-employed, however, would suggest that those choosing self-employment are less discouraged by the greater potential for variability in outcomes.[5] These individuals are more likely to be risk-loving as they are implicitly opting for a 'lottery' that may have similar average returns, but a wider range of pay-offs. Employees, by contrast, are choosing a path where the average (or expected) returns may be the same, but the range of potential outcomes is not as wide.

This seems intuitively appealing until one asks why we observe the 'losers' from self-employment continuing to work for themselves (something upon which Parker (2004) speculates). On paper many of the self-employed would be better off taking up employee jobs as they are gaining a poor reward for the skills they possess. In a free market we may expect them to move into an employee job if their gamble has clearly not paid off. This is a dynamic environment, however, where over half (53 per cent) of all new businesses in the UK are not in existence five years after

---

5   In the phraseology of economists they attribute a lower level of disutility to this
    uncertainty.

starting.[6] Clearly, we need to view self-employment and small business creation as a game or a lottery that is repeated.

More specifically, at any one point in time we may observe 'winners' and 'losers' from self-employment, but while this snapshot seems to capture the variability in returns *between* self-employed individuals, it does not capture the potential variability through time *for each* individual.[7] In a number of ways this fits with the approach of Jovanovic (1982),[8] who considers initial periods of self-employment as times of learning and discovery, with entrepreneurs finding out whether they have the appropriate skills and abilities only when they actually become self-employed. Each individual, as they undertake this process of learning, will potentially experience multiple periods of self-employment and in each period we may expect the returns to vary, as those who uncover (and bolster) a talent for self-employment experience variable, but increasing, returns, and others realise they have less of an ability and eventually exit.

Again, this would seem to fit with the evidence. In a review of studies that estimate the returns to self-employment, Carter (2009) points out that those focusing on entrepreneurial incomes often find that returns are typically lower, when compared with those for employees; in contrast, studies that have the wealth of households as the unit of analysis identify a 'tight relationship between being an entrepreneur and being rich' (Cagetti and de Nardi, 2006: 838, as cited in Carter, 2009). Similarly, Hamilton (2000) suggests that previous studies may overestimate

---

6   ONS and BIS, *Business Demography Statistics*, 2009.

7   More technically, we are capturing inter-, but not intra-, individual variability.

8   It also seems to sit with the evidence (see, for instance, Parker, 2004) that suggests previous entrepreneurial experience is a determinant of present entrepreneurial success.

the average returns to self-employment, as they seem to be falsely inflated by 'a handful of high-income entrepreneurial "superstars"'.

This may seem like inconsequential theorising, but it leads us to a number of important conclusions on the decision-making process of individuals as they choose whether to enter self-employment, and their subsequent choices over whether to persist or exit to an employee job.

Firstly, the individual faces not only uncertainty with the self-employment option but also a lack of information on the extent of that uncertainty. The suggestion that 'entrepreneurial opportunities cannot be assigned probabilities' (Blanchflower and Oswald, 1998) is an approach that can be traced back to the work of Knight (1921). The implication is that, even in cases where we would expect individuals to secure average returns from moving into self-employment that far outweigh those from an employee job, a lack of information on the nature of the self-employment 'bet' would prevent them from making well-informed decisions – that is the nature of entrepreneurship. The econometric evidence (Parker, 2004) shows that observable characteristics of the individual (such as education, experience, etc.) are much more (statistically) significant in determining employee wages in a regression equation than these characteristics are for the self-employed. This is another reflection of the relative certainty associated with the returns that flow from an employee job.[9]

Secondly, this uncertainty suggests that the only way to learn about self-employment (and your aptitude for it) is to learn 'on

---

9   There is a higher degree of correspondence between level of qualification and returns, because educational qualifications are used as signals for allocating employees to positions within institutions.

the job' (Jovanovic, 1982). As a result, even in a situation where we observe few barriers to movement between self-employment and being an employee, we observe at a point in time individuals who are persisting with self-employment, even though they would seem better served moving into an employee job. We might call this 'Del-Boy' syndrome in homage to the man who always believed that 'next year we will be millionaires' and, if we remember, does actually make it in the end.

The length of time somebody persists with this 'learning' will depend on the relative attractiveness of alternative employee jobs in each time period and the individual's personal and financial circumstances (as well as their degree of optimism[10]). We can see how some individuals might continue with self-employment for long periods, before accepting that their skills and abilities are not good enough to obtain an acceptable pay-off, never mind the 'winning prize'.

Thirdly, when observing that the wealthy are likely to have been entrepreneurs, one is simply identifying the fact that (i) for a very small few, the returns can be phenomenal and (ii) even those eventually experiencing stellar returns are likely to have been observed previously as running a failing enterprise. For those who wish to become truly wealthy, it would seem reasonable to suggest that they need to own/control the factors of production (and the rents accruing) rather than being a factor of production (an employee) themselves.[11]

---

10 See, for instance, Fraser and Greene (2004).

11 It is important to note that there is another potential interpretation, as one could argue that, having become wealthy, people are more likely to take up some form of entrepreneurship. Many researchers (following Evans and Jovanovic, 1989) find that liquidity constraints are binding (suggesting wealth impacts on entrepreneurship). Outside banking, sports and media, however, wealth would

Finally, while the previous discussion of the self-employed learning on the job hints at a potentially important role for serial entrepreneurship, it is worth emphasising that various studies detail another potential avenue for learning. Parker (2004) suggests that having parents who were themselves self-employed increases the probability that individuals will also be observed working for themselves (having controlled for other factors) – an effect that becomes even stronger if these parents had employees. While this could clearly be driven by a variety of factors, evidence suggests that parental finance is less of an influence than first-hand experience of self-employment (Dunn and Holtz-Eakin, 2000). There is also some evidence (Parker, 2004, citing the work of Boden, 1996) that employees in small firms have a greater propensity to subsequently become entrepreneurs themselves. It may be that observing entrepreneurs at work overcomes a lack of information on this form of working for many people and that they are then more likely to take it up themselves.

In Chapters 4 and 5 we return to consider the potential for entrepreneurship to be lost to the economy because individuals (perhaps wrongly) choose an employee job over the option of self-employment (simply because it is a less well-defined gamble). But, for now, we continue with a consideration of the possible reasons why we observe the opposite – individuals choosing to take up self-employment and persisting with it, even in the light of apparently poor returns. In certain sectors, such as construction, self-employed working is so extensive that individuals are likely to be much better informed of the relative risks and returns of being self-employed, as opposed to having an employee job. As we shall

seem to require a return from factors of production, rather than being a factor of production.

see in Chapter 3, however, there are still reasons to believe that in these situations we may see certain groups in society being particularly associated with self-employment, even when an employee job matching their skills and abilities would produce a higher return.

Regulation, taxation and the role of government

The fact that 36 per cent of those working in the construction sector (LFS, 2009) report themselves as being self-employed has pushed some commentators (for instance, Harvey, 1995) to argue that many are effectively employees (i.e. their working arrangements are such that they have a contract of service). As Harvey and Behling (2010) suggest, the historical cash-in-hand nature of work in the construction industry led to an essential 'endorsing [of] mass self-employment' (p. 4) with Bills in the early 1970s (most notably the Construction Industry Contracts Bill in 1970) creating two tiers of self-employed in the construction sector. There is a category of self-employed workers who have to satisfy the usual requirements that they are working under contract for services, but also a second tier who have tax deducted at source by the 'engager'. The arguments of Harvey and others are that even recent moves to alter this system have not had a significant impact and as a result many are falsely self-employed.

Arrangements in the construction sector have been considered a potential model to tackle the wider problem (see, for instance, Freedman, 2001) that stems from the differential tax treatment of the self-employed and employees. Thus, while we have suggested that such high concentrations of self-employment in particular industry sectors may reflect structural factors, it is also the case that regulations, including tax regulations, might be important.

'Pull' factors into self-employment

There are clear tax advantages to the declaration of a working relationship as being between a self-employed individual and a contractor, and this may be expected to represent an implicit policy push towards self-employment for many (HMRC, 2009). For employers the incentives stem from the fact that they are required to pay National Insurance contributions (NICs) on payments to employees, but this is not the case when they commission somebody who is self-employed. From the worker's viewpoint, being self-employed results in lower NIC payments. Also, the self-employed are taxed on profits from their business and have the opportunity to set a number of costs as deductions from taxable income. The potential savings on both sides of the employment relationship may be expected to falsely inflate the number of self-employed.

As Blanchflower (2007) suggests, in the mid-1990s the Inland Revenue's moves to clamp down on those who were perceived as using self-employment as a way of circumventing payment of NICs and other associated employee costs caused a fall in self-employment among construction workers. The continuing IR35 threat to those seen by HMRC as being falsely self-employed is likely to be a further deterrent offsetting the incentive to become self-employed purely for tax reasons.

The focus of prosecution is on the self-employed individual, not the (usually large) firm which is purchasing the goods or services. This is despite the fact that the self-employed individual (in choosing this working arrangement) forgoes holiday pay, sick leave and a variety of other benefits. Also, as Chittenden et al. (2010: 60) suggest, the self-employed incur high compliance costs associated with this form of working. In contrast, it is hard to see

The draughtsman's contract (the history of a 'freelance draffy')

During the 1970s and 1980s the pattern was that, if subcontracting to a large company, you worked through an agent, but, if working for a small company, you could usually work directly. Towards the end of the 1980s pressure was applied by the Inland Revenue to ensure that people working through agencies or companies were not avoiding taxes. Most agents looking for engineering management and design staff now required those with whom they contracted to have limited company status, with more and more companies being reluctant to deal directly with the self-employed. They were concerned that they would have to pay the contractor's tax bill if the contractor failed to file a return and accountants became worried about the type of expenses that could be offset against tax.

In the late 1990s there was a clamp-down on 'bogus' self-employment in the construction industry but a loophole allowed companies to continue using self-employed labour as long as it was provided through agencies (which would pay the National Insurance). Large companies needed only to have a small direct labour force, as they had access to a large labour pool as required. At that time some of the small building companies with whom I dealt used mainly self-employed labour-only subcontractors. They worried about how they would absorb the extra costs of working through an agency when their margins were so small. This action appeared to be the precursor to IR35. Also there were rumours around this time that some self-employed in the information technology industry were on massively inflated hourly rates and manipulating the limited company status to ensure minimum tax liability.

On 9 March 1999 the Inland Revenue issued a press release detailing how 'changes are to be introduced to counter avoidance in the area of personal service provision'. Essentially the government had identified contractors as 'tax avoiders'.

About this time I obtained a position (through an agent) as a senior mechanical design engineer with a multinational company on a £23 million project. I worked from the company's head office, where the only staff member on the project was the project manager with the remainder self-employed (myself as senior engineer, seven other engineers, three draughtsmen, office and site managers). To design, install and commission the work over eighteen months required a dedicated professional team with a high level of commitment – not a bunch of 'tax avoiders'. The company, which had several similar projects across the world, relied on self-employed labour to deliver projects. It would have been commercial suicide for a company to have a direct labour pool to service these intermittent projects. It was accepted by the project team that, as the project came to an end, the labour force would diminish. Usually a week or two's notice was given so that a contractor could approach another agency to maintain continuity of work.

Most of the project team were worried about the implications of IR35. The possibility of an Inland Revenue investigation removing one's self-employed status and making you liable for unpaid taxes over previous years was daunting. We considered that we were providing an essential service to the engineering industry. Yes, we received a higher remuneration than direct labour but received none of the staff benefits, i.e. paid holidays, sick pay, pension scheme, redundancy payment, etc. All of us employed an accountant (who had a reputation to maintain) to ensure that our tax returns complied with existing Inland Revenue policy. Some of the project team, frightened by the implications of IR35, joined 'umbrella' Ltd companies that had found a loophole in the legislation. For a small fee they would deal with all your remuneration and liabilities as a self-employed person but also guarantee you protection from the ravages of the Inland Revenue. Some other self-employed became staff members.

About ten years ago I and a fellow draughtsman received (separate) correspondence from the Inland Revenue disputing our status as self-employed persons working through a limited company. In both cases, this initial charge from the Inland Revenue was overturned (following correspondence, various meetings, production of evidence and payments to consultants). We both experienced a considerable amount of stress, my colleague had to pay out £1,500 in consultancy and accountant fees, he lost income while attending meetings and the outcome of my investigation was that my status was accepted but I received an extra tax bill for £70, which I paid. The following year I received a rebate of £70.

Surely, rather than chasing little fish such as myself from which the returns are minimal, the Inland Revenue should be chasing big companies if they truly wish to change employment practices.

Based on an interview with self-employed person

what the employer loses from using a self-employment relationship as cover for a normal employer/employer relationship and, in sectors such as construction, where a few large firms dominate, there would seem to be a greater ability of firms to dictate working relationships.

As Crawford and Freedman (2010) suggest, the increasing ease with which individuals have been able to create companies and therefore become incorporated has further widened the potential gap between the tax treatment of the self-employed and employees. Creating companies provides an opportunity to characterise labour income as income from capital. Furthermore, as it has become easier and more attractive (from a taxation perspective) to set up as a self-employed person running an incorporated firm, it has arguably become more costly for firms to go down the employee route.

'Push' factors out of employment

Redston (2004) argues that both the increasing cost of NICs and the extensions to employment protection legislation (EPL) have increased the costs associated with a company taking on an additional employee and therefore increased the levels of self-employment (see also Nicoletti and Scarpetta, 1999). Just as the favourable tax treatment of the self-employed can be thought of as an artificial 'pull' factor into self-employment, EPL can be thought of as an artificial 'push' factor out of employment. This factor will work through reducing employment opportunities to individuals who may then become self-employed; it will also prompt employers of all sizes to consider outsourcing and engaging in contract for services, rather than a contract of service (Robson, 2003).

The first aspect of this argument fits with the push–pull framework already mentioned – individuals would turn to self-employment as an alternative, in the face of reduced opportunities for employee jobs. The latter effect could manifest itself in various ways, however. For example, employers might also use employees on temporary contracts or use agency workers rather than reorganise their business model around self-employment and contracting for services. It should be noted, though, that the remit of EPL has grown to encompass many of these more flexible forms of working.

Impact on self-employment and job creation of other forms of regulation

It is also to be expected that increasing product market regulation (PMR) will raise barriers to entry, as compliance with such regulations becomes a cost of entering and supplying the product. This will be expected, all other things being equal, to raise the minimum average size of firms in the affected industry. A special issue of the *Economic Journal* (2007)[12] suggests that the interactions between PMR and EPL cause particular problems for small firms. There is also a suggestion that there is a direct impact of EPL, which differs by firm and worker type; including the suggestion that EPL drives small firms out of the market.

How do these various countervailing pressures jointly impact on the self-employed and the jobs they create? To clarify this, we need to distinguish between the self-employed with, and those without, employees. This is best expressed in a distinction drawn

---

12   See, for instance, the feature article, Cahuc and Koeniger (2007).

by some of the respondents (in Portugal and the UK) from the International Organisation of Employers' study.[13] This distinction is that respondents in those countries found that while establishing an enterprise was straightforward, developing the business (once it was up and running) was impeded by regulatory constraints on growth. This can lead to an interesting situation, which we may observe in the UK. Becoming self-employed may be relatively easy and, indeed, advantageous because of the tax and regulatory regime. It may then be difficult for the self-employed to develop their businesses and take on more employees. Both these effects may increase self-employment but that increase in self-employment would not be indicative of a thriving enterprise society.

Generally, the combined incentives of the tax system represent an inducement to individuals and firms to consider self-employment (without employees) as an alternative to being an employee. EPL would seem to have the potential to provide a further push towards self-employment without employees (as it has the potential to 'dampen' down new employee job opportunities, in the face of increased product demand). At the same time, however, EPL and the compliance costs of the PAYE system (Chittenden et al., 2005: 639) make the self-employed without employees less inclined to take on employees.

The overall effect is to incentivise self-employment without employees, but also to place barriers to the expansion of these businesses through the employment of others. If we further consider the role of PMR, there would seem to be the potential for a squeezing of firms with very few employees – the potential

13   International Organisation of Employers, *Labour Law and Micro and Small Enterprises Survey*, November 2006.

combined effects are to push the distribution of firms towards the extremes of (i) self-employed with no employees and (ii) a rising average size of firm among those with employees. The analysis of BIS data in Chapter 1 suggests that this is quite a good description of UK enterprises over the last decade, though we have not proved a direct causal link.

Access to finance

One of the main potential barriers to those considering self-employment is the lack of finance. The increased personal equity resulting from a booming housing market and the possibility that financial liberalisation leads to easier credit and lowers the returns required from business investments (see, for instance, Taylor, 1996; Blanchflower et al., 2003) have been put forward as potential explanations for rising levels of self-employment.

Roper et al. (2006) examine the evidence on sources of funding for small businesses and the self-employed, attempting to split this into either demand or supply-side explanations.[14] For instance, evidence on the supply side suggests that bank loans constitute one source of funding for two-thirds of UK businesses (Cosh and Hughes, 2003) and for a quarter of these firms this is the largest single component of funding. Considering the demand from SMEs for finance, however, Fraser (2005) suggests that (before the present downturn) 65 per cent of start-ups drew on personal savings; only 10 per cent relied on bank loans and 6 per cent on friends and family. There is an extensive literature on the apparent unwillingness of many banks to lend to SMEs, because

14   In this they take the direction of Kotey (1999).

of the perceived risks (ibid.) and in the present downturn this has become a particularly hot political issue. It would seem to have created more heat than light, however.

The crisis is, at its root, one of a failure of confidence across the financial sector, with poorly performing loans/financial products at its heart. Politicians have been encouraging banks to lend to small businesses, but banks would seemingly need to relax their lending criteria to increase the supply of funding to small businesses, as they are more likely to fail. Many commentators perceive an important role for entrepreneurs as drivers of economic growth, and in the present environment the imperative of banks and other financial institutions to improve the performance of their loan portfolios may therefore be seen as a particular drag on future growth prospects.

It is important to note that high average failure rates are not in themselves a problem. Banks have sophisticated methods for the scoring of risk, which aim to differentiate the good from the bad bets. The problem here, however, is that the risk-scoring methodologies that are used for prediction of financial default in the banking and insurance sectors (Parnitzke, 2005; Kraft, Kroisandt and Muller, 2002) rely on being able to make relatively accurate predictions using approaches such as linear discriminant analysis and logistic regression (Altman, 1968; Aker, 2004). As we will see in Chapter 4, the academic community is still unable to accurately model small business/self-employment success and failure, and it is unlikely that the techniques used by the banks are any more sophisticated. There is still, therefore, a great deal of both risk and uncertainty surrounding any particular loan to a small business.

In such situations banks and other funding institutions demand greater collateral (see Blanchflower and Oswald, 1998) and also use a variety of indicators to screen ventures. Unfortunately, there is the potential here for the same sorts of barriers to the securing of funding for new ventures as there are for the barriers to obtaining an employee job. When the main indicators of potential small business and self-employment success are unobservable, lenders attempt to discriminate between good and bad bets using observable characteristics. For instance, Bates (1990) finds that educational qualifications are a major determinant of the financial capital structure of small business start-ups. Similarly, the need for collateral is likely to limit access to funding for expansion for many disadvantaged groups.

Barriers to finance can act to reinforce some of the effects of regulation, legislation and other 'push' factors described earlier. In the next chapter we shall see that there are a number of characteristics of the self-employed (for instance, lower levels of educational attainment) that suggest they take up self-employment because of barriers they face to obtaining an appropriate employee position. The same characteristics that 'push' individuals into self-employment, however, are likely to be those that act as a barrier to the securing of finance, if and when these individuals wish to expand their operations and take on plant or employees.[15] Aspects of the economic environment have the potential to push individuals into forms of self-employment where they face barriers to expansion – whether this is in the form of working without employees and/or a lack of funds for development of the firm.

The considerations here are somewhat different from those relating to the role played by venture capitalists in entrepreneurial

15   The fact that only 10 per cent of start-ups consider finance as a barrier (Fraser, 2005) would seem to reflect the fact that, for the roughly three-quarters who begin as self-employed without employees, capital requirements are not extensive.

success stories. One of the advantages possessed by the USA, and which is often attributed to the success of Israel in producing more than its share of entrepreneurial firms, is well-developed venture capital markets. While the situation is likely to have changed, in 2005 it was estimated that companies which had been backed by venture capitalists in some way accounted for almost 17 per cent of GDP and 9 per cent of private sector employment in the USA (*IHS Global Insight*, as quoted in Economist, 2009).

While this sounds impressive, venture capital still supports only a small percentage of start-ups (about one in every 1,000 – even in the USA). The GEM (2009) report suggests that across Europe 'only 594 seed stage companies received venture capital in 2008'. In most cases start-ups rely on friends, fools and families (or 'the three f's', as suggested in Economist, 2009). Despite the fact that we have a number of outstanding examples of successful ventures started with the three f's (Sergey Brin and Larry Page founded Google with no help from the venture capital sector), if the venture capital sector is good at picking winners then those start-ups will make a relatively large contribution to the economy.

Annex: Statistical analysis of the self-employed/ employee distinction

In this chapter we have tried to establish how the following factors are important in the self-employment decision:

- the desire to become self-employed across the population;
- the factors that will then determine whether we observe an individual choosing to become self-employed;

• the potential impact arising from 'frictions' or government policy intervention.

A sophisticated statistical analysis was undertaken by the author, the detailed results of which are available on request.[16] The analysis was designed to find out which factors are most important in determining whether we observe an individual being self-employed or in an employee job and used a technique known as binomial logit regression.

The findings were broadly compatible with the prior theory discussed above, but there were also some findings which supplemented the findings of existing studies. First, with respect to education, some studies find evidence that education is positively associated with self-employment while others suggest that there is a negative relationship between education and self-employment (Brown et al., 2007). Our study found that, relative to those who report their highest qualification as A-level or equivalent (which in the present environment can be considered as somewhere in the middle of the educational distribution), those with both higher (degree, etc.) and lower (NVQ and GCSE, etc.) categories of educational attainment are statistically significantly less likely to be self-employed. This is perhaps surprising, and there is no obvious explanation.

The inclusion of industry variables fits very much with our discussions above. Self-employment was associated with particularly large and significant coefficients for particular industries such as construction. Women are significantly less likely to be observed in self-employment, relative to having an employee

---

16   Email address: urwinp@westminster.ac.uk.

job, and older age groups are significantly more likely to be self-employed. It seems, indeed, that the rate of increase in self-employment with age does not decrease with age.

Having dependants under the age of sixteen makes one more likely to be self-employed, but there is no significant influence of marriage or cohabiting on self-employment. It is interesting to note that, having controlled for a variety of other factors, Pakistani, Bangladeshi and Chinese individuals are significantly more likely to be self-employed, when compared to their 'white British and white other' counterparts (something that we return to in the next chapter).

Generally, we find that individuals working in the south of the country are significantly more likely to be observed working as self-employed, compared with those in the north – this might partly reflect the extent of public sector employment. As one would expect, those who own their house outright are more likely to be observed working as a self-employed individual, when compared to those with a mortgage.

We cannot, of course, be sure that there is a direct causal link between our covariants and the dependent variable – for instance, finding that those who own their home outright are more likely to be self-employed could work in two ways. We could be observing the fact that those with capital are more likely to start up as self-employed or we might be observing the fact that the self-employed make more money and can therefore afford to buy their own house. Similarly, while the estimated model is relatively standard in the literature (see, for instance, Parker, 2004: 25–6), we must be aware that the specification fails to differentiate entry and survival effects. We are not modelling those who decide to become self-employed and we are not modelling those who 'survive' in self-employment – rather we are modelling a snapshot of both of these at a particular point in time. This occurs in all analyses, but because (as we have already suggested) the self-employed have particularly high rates of churn, it matters more.

These results do not help us understand the pull–push issue but they do demonstrate that certain groups in the population have a propensity towards self-employment. Whether this is because of a lack of job opportunities as employees is beside the point – it is important that self-employment opportunities are not closed off to those groups whose participation in the labour market particularly depends on self-employment. Self-employment would appear to be an important labour market option for groups (older people, certain ethnic groups) whose participation in the labour market is otherwise lower than average.

3 DISADVANTAGE, THE SELF-EMPLOYED AND THEIR EMPLOYEES

In Chapter 2 it was suggested that for most individuals self-employment might not be attractive when compared with an employee job because of the potential variability in earnings – though self-employment has the potential for higher returns and is correlated with wealth. For many, however, *appropriate* or *acceptable* employee-job opportunities may be so limited that self-employment becomes a much more attractive proposition.

The nature of firms' relationships with their employees has become more complicated over time – the control exerted by firms has increased and the position of employees has become increasingly protected. Indeed, employees in studies of labour market regulation are often described as *insiders*[1] and those who are unable to find employee jobs *outsiders.* Partly because of employment protection legislation (EPL), the criteria that employers use to screen potential employees have become increasingly stringent.[2] For many these represent substantial barriers to obtaining an employee job – even if they actually have the skills and abilities to perform the required tasks, they may not possess the relevant certificates, experience and other required 'signals' to

---

1   Lindbeck and Snower (1988).

2   In response to an asymmetry of information that exists, where the employee knows that they are lazy/motivated, but the employer does not, in a situation where EPL raises the costs of ending the employment relationship.

demonstrate that to potential employers. For example, Friedberg (2000) suggests that immigrants possessing overseas qualifications receive significantly lower returns, when compared with the equivalent qualifications gained in the country of destination.

These individuals may consider that they are a good match to a large number of employee-job opportunities, but they simply do not possess the relevant signals to be considered. In these scenarios setting up one's own business (with no employees) is the only way for an individual to supply their labour to the market at a level consummate with their underlying skills and abilities.

In this situation we may expect to observe certain groups, who are often considered to face a disadvantage in the labour market, being more likely to become self-employed. We begin this chapter by discussing ethnicity, immigration and religion: characteristics that have formed a substantial focus of the discussions on the issues of 'push and pull' within self-employment. We then discuss more specific groups of disadvantaged individuals – those for whom language is a problem in securing and retaining a job and the unemployed. This is followed by an examination of the differing nature of the employee job opportunities created by the self-employed (more specifically small and medium-sized enterprises – SMEs). This chapter concludes with a discussion of further results from multivariate analyses of self-employment. This analysis looks in more detail at the split between employees, the self-employed and the self-employed with employees.

Ethnicity, immigration and religion

There is extensive evidence (see, for instance, Blackaby et al., 1998) to suggest that Britain's ethnic minority groups suffer disadvantage in the labour market, in terms both of securing a job and of being obliged to accept a wage that is lower than that of a similarly qualified white worker. Traditionally, studies have measured the extent of this disadvantage in the form of a wage gap that cannot be explained by observable characteristics. Much of the literature, particularly in the USA, focuses on the proportion of this gap that can be attributed to labour market and pre-labour-market discrimination (Neal and Johnson,1996); with new studies using audit pair methods (Bertrand and Mullainathan, 2004) adding another dimension to the debate (Heckman, 1998).

Furthermore, within the UK, research that simply distinguishes ethnicity using the categories 'white' and 'black' misses a lot of variability, and Table 3 suggests that this is also the case for self-employment. White and white British groups have roughly average self-employment. Some ethnic groups have self-employment rates that are substantially greater than average (for example, Pakistani and Chinese). Pakistanis have traditionally been seen as a group who have faced hardships in the UK labour market (partly because of their historical association with the declining textile industry), and this may be seen as a driver of their high rates of self-employment. This explanation does not fit with the experience of Bangladeshis, however, whose rate of self-employment is similar to that for the white group, but who are also often identified as being particularly disadvantaged in many studies (see, for instance, Crawford et al., 2008).

We can get an idea of how the picture varies by gender and also how things have been changing over time, if we consider the work of Clark and Drinkwater (see, for instance, Clark and Drinkwater, 2000, 2007a, 2007b), who use data from two census surveys in 1991 and 2001. Table 4 (reproduced from Clark and

Table 3 **Employees and self-employment by ethnicity in the UK**

	White and White British	Mixed	Indian	Pakistani	Bangladeshi	Other Asian	Black Caribbean	Black African	Chinese	Other	Total
Employee	22,592,142	187,791	569,363	211,553	107,264	220,356	232,271	285,654	98,964	362,109	24,873,864
	86.8%	89.7%	88.1%	72.8%	86.2%	89.3%	92.7%	90.4%	81.5%	87.7%	86.8%
Self-employed	3,449,329	21,599	76,980	79,214	17,205	26,523	18,416	30,496	22,448	50,832	3,794,251
	13.3%	10.3%	11.9%	27.2%	13.8%	10.7%	7.4%	9.6%	18.5%	12.3%	13.2%
Total	26,041,471	209,390	646,343	290,767	124,469	246,879	250,687	316,150	121,412	412,941	28,668,115

Source: Quarterly *Labour Force Survey*, April–June 2009

Drinkwater's work for the Joseph Rowntree Foundation, 2007b) suggests that the variability observed in Table 3 is not a recent phenomenon; and census data also suggest that Pakistani, Indian and Chinese rates of self-employment are higher than those for the white group. It is interesting, however, that while the figures from Clark and Drinkwater suggest relatively high levels of Indian entrepreneurship for men and women (which also corresponds to the average for all groups), the more recent *Labour Force Survey* (LFS) figures suggest otherwise. Rates of self-employment were increasing for all groups of men apart from Indians between 1991 and 2001, and it would seem that the rate of decline in the proportion of self-employed among this group has accelerated. While the rates of self-employment seen among women tend to be much lower in general, this is still a relatively important form of working among Chinese women.

What is surprising (and perhaps calls into question the figures from the LFS for this group) is the apparent increase in self-employment among those who trace their origin to Pakistan. Other than this, however, Clark and Drinkwater (2007b) take their results as suggesting something of a convergence during the 1990s across different ethnic minority groups, with some movement away from self-employment for second-generation Indians and Chinese. Given the improvements in educational outcomes and university participation rates among ethnic minority groups in the last decade (see, for instance, Urwin et al., 2010) the convergence in self-employment rates may reflect a similar convergence in general labour market prospects. More generally, factors that may explain differences include evidence that access to capital differs according to ethnic group (Parker, 2004). Clark and Drinkwater (2007a) also suggest that ethnic minority individuals who

Table 4 **Self-employment rates among male and female ethnic minority groups**

	Male		Female	
	1991	2001	1991	2001
White	13%	14%	4%	5%
Pakistani	16%	18%	3%	3%
Black Caribbean	6%	9%	1%	2%
Bangladeshi	10%	12%	1%	1%
Black African	8%	10%	2%	3%
Chinese	22%	23%	13%	12%
Indian	19%	17%	7%	7%

Source: Clark and Drinkwater (2007b) using 1991 and 2001 census data

have a preference for 'ethnic residential segregation' do not do as well as those with more integrated living patterns.

It would seem that the only obvious explanation for this varying pattern of self-employment among ethnic minority groups is the existence of cultural 'pull' factors alongside the usual 'push' and 'pull' factors that tend to exist. Even in this more disaggregated analysis, however, we are still missing out on a lot of potential variation – for instance, grouping the quarter of a million 'other Asians' together, as well as missing the variability in backgrounds among the 'white and white British'. While ethnicity may be a factor in determining labour market outcomes, there are other factors that are likely to be driving the take-up of self-employment, which may be correlated with ethnicity, but which may provide a better explanation for the variability.

For instance, the LFS allows us to identify over two hundred different countries of birth for respondents, and Table 5 sets out the varying rates of self-employment observed among those from

Table 5 **The proportion of employees and self-employed according to their country of birth**

	Northern Europe	Southern Europe	Eastern Europe	Balkans, USSR, Russia, Caucasus, Turkey*	UK	North Americ
Employee	455,044	186,411	476,469	58,875	21,721,109	116,714
	85.97%†	84.98%	80.99%	75.56%	87.05%	85.51%
Self-employed	74,275	32,942	111,804	19,039	3,232,136	19,771
	14.03%	15.02%	19.01%	24.44%	12.95%	14.49%
Total	529,319	219,353	588,273	77,914	24,953,245	136,485
	100%	100%	100%	100%	100%	100%

* The figures for this group are boosted by those whose country of birth is Turkey, but cell size does not allow separate analysis of this group.

† % of those in employment. For ease, unpaid family workers have not been included. Consideration of this latter group, however, or inclusion of those who are not in employment, does not change the general findings

§ The small number of Chinese in this group who have self-employment rates of 23% does not offset the generally lower levels seen amongst this group.

Source: Quarterly *Labour Force Survey*, April–June 2009

various (grouped) regions of the world. As the notes to the table suggest, even this level of disaggregation is unhelpful in some cases (for instance, those in the UK whose country of origin is either China or Turkey). A comparison of the rates of self-employment between all those born outside of the UK (15 per cent) and those born in the UK (13 per cent), however, suggests that the former tend to have higher rates of self-employment.

As already suggested, this could reflect more limited access to appropriate employee job opportunities (perhaps because of language issues or a lack of perceived equivalence of qualifications gained abroad). Once again, however, any such overall immigrant/native gap in Table 5 seems small compared with the variability across different immigrant groups. Furthermore, this would not seem to be simply a case of those from less developed

Central and South America	Caribbean	Africa	Middle East	Central Asia	East and South Asia[§]	Australia, etc.	Total
71,908	102,719	612,934	70,619	556,694	308,017	118,230	24,855,743
81.32%	92.19%	88.73%	81.37%	81.09%	90.02%	86.46%	86.76%
16,518	8,696	77,863	16,169	129,815	34,132	18,517	3,791,677
18.68%	7.81%	11.27%	18.63%	18.91%	9.98%	13.54%	13.24%
88,426	111,415	690,797	86,788	686,509	342,149	136,747	28,647,420
100%	100%	100%	100%	100%	100%	100%	100%

countries (where self-employment is generally higher) bringing a greater understanding of entrepreneurship to the UK. Though there would seem to be something of this effect at work, this does not explain the exceptionally high rates of self-employment among those born in Turkey, for example, when compared with the low rates for those born in Africa.

It would appear that, on average, first-generation immigrants tend to have higher rates of self-employment than second and subsequent generations, and this is confirmed by evidence elsewhere (Clark and Drinkwater, 2007a). Studies that consider the potential for this to be driven by differing cultural and religious attitudes to entrepreneurship (Bonin et al., 2006), however, do not identify the sort of substantial differences that would be needed to explain differences in observed self-employment rates.

Table 6 is able to shed more light on this with an analysis of the varying rates of self-employment according to the reported religion of a respondent. This is a relatively new way of being able to look at rates of self-employment, as questions on religion have not traditionally been widely asked in the UK (though the LFS has been asking all respondents to detail their religion since spring 2004). Once again we can see how the majority (in this case Christian) group have lower levels of self-employment (12.7 per cent), compared with a rate of 16.8 per cent for all other religions. This is perhaps a more pronounced differential than that seen elsewhere, and it is interesting that there is a significant difference between those with adherence to Jewish and Muslim faiths who have particularly high rates of self-employment (30.1 per cent and 20.1 per cent respectively) and those who adhere to the Hindu and Sikh faiths (10.6 per cent and 12.7 per cent respectively). We can see a clear potential role here for cultural pull factors.

While this discussion has been couched in terms of 'push–pull', what it seems to highlight is the potential social role that self-employment plays in many communities. We do seem to be observing a situation where groups who suffer some form of disadvantage (in terms of barriers to an employee job) have higher average levels of self-employment; but that religion and culture interact with this in a way that results in differing levels of self-employment and entrepreneurship. It is also notable that while the *Household Survey of Entrepreneurship* (DTI Small Business Service, 2005) identifies a higher proportion of individuals in certain ethnic minority groups who are thinking of starting up their own enterprise, these tend to be the groups from Tables 3 and 4 that have lower rates of self-employment. This may suggest a general greater propensity to consider self-employment across

Table 6 **Proportions of employees and self-employed among those of differing religions in the UK, 2009**

	N/A	Christian	Buddhist	Hindu	Jewish	Muslim	Sikh	Any other	No religion	Total
Employee	652,492	17,457,168	94,499	346,669	102,240	598,960	154,807	224,106	5,242,923	24,873,864
	84.6%	87.3%	84.1%	89.4%	69.9%	79.9%	87.3%	80.6%	86.8%	86.8%
Self-employed	118,630	2,544,763	17,909	41,239	43,933	150,381	22,566	54,073	800,757	3,794,251
	15.4%	12.7%	15.9%	10.6%	30.1%	20.1%	12.7%	19.4%	13.3%	13.2%
Total frequency	771,122	20,001,931	112,408	387,908	146,173	749,341	177,373	278,179	6,043,680	28,668,115

Source: Quarterly *Labour Force Survey*, April–June 2009

Table 7 **Proportions of respondents in various economic activity categories twelve months ago, according to whether they are now self-employed or employees**

		Employment status 12 months ago							
	N/A	Working in paid job or business	Unemployed or 'not in waged employment'**	Full-time student	Looking after family or home	Long-term sick or disabled	Retired	None of these	Total
Employee at present time	3,894,278	19,508,092	360,086	663,113	170,173	46,755	36,204	195,163	24,873,864
	87.05%	86.53%	87.77%	97.37%	81.15%	85.59%	71.65%	80.41%	86.76%
Self-employed at present time	579,108	3,037,789	50,173	17,906	39,525	7,872	14,322	47,556	3,794,251
	12.95%	13.47%	12.23%	2.63%	18.85%	14.41%	28.35%	19.59%	13.24%
Total	4,473,386	22,545,881	410,259	681,019	209,698	54,627	50,526	242,719	28,668,115

* The latter group includes those who twelve months ago were (i) laid off or on short time, (ii) unpaid family workers or (iii) on special government schemes

Source: Quarterly *Labour Force Survey*, April–June 2009

ethnic minority groups, but one that is tempered by issues of 'access' to self-employment itself (see below).

Unemployment, inactivity and language

There are other examples of self-employment being important for groups who may be at a disadvantage in the labour market. Most of the research in this area has been undertaken in the USA (see, for instance, Fairlie, 2005). Studies undertaken in the UK include Bryson and White (1996); and Reize (2000) has taken a similar approach with data on unemployed Germans.

Unfortunately the cross-sectional nature of the LFS does not allow us to follow the unemployed for a long enough period of time to track their use of self-employment as a ladder of opportunity.[3] When we consider datasets such as the British Household Panel Survey (BHPS), which follow a group of individuals through time and could be used for such purposes, the numbers of unemployed that we can observe who, in addition, become self-employed becomes too small.

Having said this, the LFS does allow some insight, and Table 7 presents interesting evidence on the present employment status of respondents according to their activity twelve months previously (the results are for April–June 2009). As we can see, of those who were unemployed or not in waged employment twelve months previously, self-employment is an important route into employment, but at 12.2 per cent it is still the case that a smaller

---

3   The LFS does have a five-quarter rolling panel element – with each quarter being made up of a fifth for whom it will be their first interview; a fifth for whom it will be their second interview, and so on. While pooling of these different waves would boost the overall panel sample size, being able to follow individuals for just over one year would not provide enormous additional insights.

Table 8 **The split of self-employment with and without employees according to main economic activity status twelve months ago**

	N/A	Working in paid job or business	Unemployed or 'not in waged employment'*	Full-time student	Looking after family or home	Long-term sick or disabled	Retired	None of these	Total
On own or with a partner (no employees)	437,987 75.87%	2,391,711 78.77%	47,260 94.19%	16,822 93.95%	36,648 92.72%	7,872 100%	12,745 88.99%	43,284 91.02%	2,994,329 78.98%
With employees	139,305 24.13%	644,674 21.23%	2,913 5.81%	1,084 6.05%	2,877 7.28%	0 0%	1,577 11.01%	4,272 8.98%	796,702 21.02%
Total	577,292	3,036,385	50,173	17,906	39,525	7,872	14,322	47,556	3,791,031

* The latter group includes those who twelve months ago were (i) laid off or on short time, (ii) unpaid family workers or (iii) on special government schemes

Source: Quarterly *Labour Force Survey*, April–June 2009

proportion of the unemployed become self-employed than are self-employed in the population as a whole. When we consider other groups who, twelve months previously, were not in waged employment, however, virtually all of them (apart from students) have rates of self-employment higher than the average for the UK – this is particularly interesting to note for the group that report 'none of these' as their activity status twelve months ago, who may be taken as NEETs (Not in Education, Employment or Training).

In previous chapters we have hinted at the need to distinguish between the self-employed with and without employees. From our discussion of push factors, access to finance, the potential impacts of EPL and the wider regulatory burden, it would seem reasonable to suggest that self-employment which is acting as a gateway to employment would be of the kind that is without employees. As Table 8 suggests, in the case of the groups shown above in Table 7, this is very much the case – the numbers starting up as self-employed with employees are so small they render cell sizes unreliable. This perhaps seems obvious, but relatively few studies make the distinction between self-employed with and without employees (though see later discussions of Cowling et al., 2004).

Despite some indication that the disadvantaged use self-employment as a route to employment, within this literature there is still no consensus on its value as a pathway to a more secure labour market profile. The debate tends to focus on a perceived trade-off between high failure rates among small business start-ups, as opposed to some findings that 'better'[4] workers seem particularly likely to take up self-employment. For instance, the

---

4   In Bryson and White (1996) 'better' refers to those with more favourable employment histories, though the authors do suggest that some evidence of these workers being 'pushed' into self-employment may be apparent.

work of Holtz-Eakin et al. (2000) in the USA seems to suggest that self-employment may improve upward mobility for those on low incomes and has the opposite effect for high-income Americans. In contrast, evidence from Spain suggests that exit rates from self-employment for the unemployed were three times higher than for previously employed males (Carrasco, 1999, cited in Parker, 2004).

There are questions, however, over the appropriateness of comparator groups in some studies – we would wish to compare unemployed individuals with similar characteristics who move into (i) self-employment and (ii) an employee job. Evidence from Lofstrom (2009) using groups of similarly low-skilled (but not unemployed) individuals suggests that the returns to self-employed men are relatively high, but that low-skilled women do better in waged employment. Whatever the pros and cons with respect to the unemployed it would seem that many groups who experience a period outside of employment use self-employment as a way of returning – and this particularly manifests itself as self-employment without employees.

In subsequent sections of this monograph, the focus of discussion is on the self-employed with employees (or more accurately, in the next section, the employees of small businesses), but before moving on to consideration of this group, one last piece of evidence gives some insight into how much more complicated the issue of disadvantage can be with respect to self-employment. Table 9 sets out the rates of self-employment according to the response of men in the LFS who report that English is, or is not, the language spoken at home.[5]

5   Note that the quarter we are using has changed, as language questions are asked only in July to September quarters of the LFS.

The focus on men is driven by existing evidence (see, for instance, Crawford et al., 2008) on the particular variability in female participation rates, due to cultural and language factors, across different ethnic groups. What Table 9 suggests is that men not speaking English at home do have some greater propensity to be self-employed, though the gap between English and 'other' (which is all languages other than English and the Celtic languages) is small.

Table 9 **Self-employment among men according to main language spoken at home**

	English	Welsh, Gaelic, Ulster Scots, Ullans	Other	Total
Employee	10,214,703	45,886	741,564	11,002,153
	83%	70%	81%	82%
Self-employed	2,156,149	19,921	170,407	2,346,477
	17%	30%	19%	18%
Total	12,370,852	65,807	911,971	13,348,630
Total, including inactive	19,843,433	113,415	1,343,836	21,300,684

Source: Quarterly *Labour Force Survey*, July–September 2009

We would perhaps expect to observe individuals who live in a home where English is not the main language to have higher levels of self-employment. When we dig down into this in more detail, however, there is a more nuanced picture. Table 10 considers the 1.3 million people from Table 9 who respond that an 'other' language is spoken at home and asks whether language is a barrier to obtaining and/or keeping a job. When considering the broader picture, which incorporates both the economically active and the economically inactive, Table 10 shows how the percentage of self-employment and employee jobs among men who report language as a problem (10.4 per cent and 49.4 per cent respectively) is lower than among those who report that it is not a problem (56.2 per cent and 13 per cent). The suggestion is that, while we may consider disadvantage as a driver of self-employment, being too disadvantaged may result in lower levels of both self-employment and employee jobs, as individuals simply cannot 'access' the labour market in any form – or cannot obtain remuneration higher than benefit levels.

Table 10 **Self-employment among men according to whether they have language difficulties in getting/keeping a job**

	No answer	Yes, language is a problem	No, language is not a problem	Total
Employee	2,866	91,249	647,449	741,564
	45.75%	49.39%	56.16%	52.50%
Self-employed	1,473	19,193	149,741	170,407
	23.52%	10.39%	12.99%	11.32%
Govt-trained and	0	567	6,728	7,295
unpaid family workers (UFW)	0%	0.31%	0.58%	0.38%
Unemployed	829	22,520	93,367	116,716
	13.23%	12.19%	8.10%	8.69%
Inactive, seeking	0	1,406	5,091	6,497
	0%	0.76%	0.44%	0.49%
Inactive, not seeking	1,096	49,817	250,444	301,357
	17.50%	26.96%	21.72%	22.43%
Total	6,264	184,752	1,152,820	1,343,836

Source: Quarterly *Labour Force Survey*, July–September 2009

The employees of the self-employed

It is also possible that the employees of the self-employed have characteristics that are very different from those seen among employees in larger firms. Unfortunately, it is not possible for us to directly observe individuals who report that they work for the self-employed in surveys such as the LFS.[6] Therefore, we consider the extent to which there are systematic differences in the characteristics of employees in firms of different sizes. Once again, the underlying assumption is that the self-employed with employees predominate among micro-businesses and then, as we move up through small and into medium-sized firms, enterprises are less and less likely to be run by owner-managers.

Table 11 begins by looking at the sex breakdown of employees among firms of different sizes. Overall, the suggestion is that the proportion of women in firms of fewer than 50 employees is over 50 per cent, whereas among firms larger than this less than half of the workforce is female. Table 11 does not present a consistent pattern of falling proportions of female workers in steadily larger firms, but this is not perhaps surprising, as there is a potential for sector differences to blur any such clarity. For instance, it could be the case that small firms are more likely to be located within certain sectors, such as manufacturing, where we are less likely to observe female employees in either large or small firms.

Further analysis suggests that this is confounding the picture somewhat, and when we consider particular sectors, gender differences are even more pronounced. For instance, in the *Financial and Insurance* activities sector, where women make up

---

6   It is unlikely that many respondents would be able to differentiate the status of the business owner, especially given the problems over a clear legal/regulatory distinction.

Table 11 **The gender distribution of employees according to firm size (measured by number of employees)**

| | Firm size according to number of employees | | | | | | | | Self-employed | |
	1–10	11–24	25–49	50–249	DNK but 50–499	250–499	500+	Total	Without employees	With employees
Male	2,258,766	1,745,454	1,545,640	3,118,973	441,936	1,039,295	2,306,145	12,456,209	2,106,066	604,568
	48.59%	47.1%	46.17%	53.8%	58.24%	56.45%	51.3%	50.65%	70.34%	75.88%
Female	2,390,130	1,960,168	1,802,339	2,677,972	316,837	801,743	2,188,927	12,138,116	888,263	192,134
	51.41%	52.9%	53.83%	46.2%	41.76%	43.55%	48.7%	49.35%	29.66%	24.12%
Total	4,648,896	3,705,622	3,347,979	5,796,945	758,773	1,841,038	4,495,072	24,594,325	2,994,329	796,702

Source: Quarterly *Labour Force Survey*, April–June 2009. DNK = do not know.

Table 12 **Part-time and full-time employees according to firm size**

| | Firm size according to number of employees | | | | | | | |
	1–10	11–24	25–49	50–249	DNK but 50–499	250–499	500+	Total
Full-time	2,915,612	2,495,394	2,412,697	4,554,457	587,118	1,489,849	3,734,778	18,189,905
	62.72%	67.34%	72.06%	78.57%	77.38%	80.92%	83.09%	73.96%
Part-time	1,731,298	1,210,228	933,287	1,241,375	171,655	350,720	758,537	6,397,100
	37.24%	32.66%	27.88%	21.41%	22.62%	19.05%	16.87%	26.01%
Total	4,648,896	3,705,622	3,347,979	5,796,945	758,773	1,841,038	4,495,072	24,594,325

Source: Quarterly *Labour Force Survey*, April–June 2009. DNK = do not know.

approximately 50 per cent of overall employment, 65 per cent of employees in the smallest firms are female compared with 45 per cent in the largest. The pattern is very similar in sectors where women dominate, such as education – women make up 75 per cent of overall employment, but while we observe 80 per cent of employees being female in the smallest firms, the figure for the largest is only 53 per cent. Across many sectors, it appears that the smallest firms have a propensity to employ female workers.

It is possible that the nature of employment in small and large firms within the same industry could be different, and this could explain differential patterns in female working. Table 12 suggests one such explanation, as sex differences are also reflected in patterns of part-time and full-time working. If smaller firms are more likely to be offering flexible working practices, and women are more likely to take these up, then this may be a cause of the differences between male and female employment patterns across small and large firms. The question still remains, however, as to why we observe these differences in working practices, and to take this forward further we move away from sex differences to consider whether other patterns of employee demography differ by firm size.

For instance, Table 13 sets out the age distribution of employees according to the same categories of firm size. The proportion of employees in larger firms who are 'prime aged' (25–39 or 40–49) is 67 per cent, compared with only 54 per cent in the smallest firms. As we move up the size distribution of firms, we are less likely to observe both the oldest and youngest employees.

It is important to remind ourselves that, together with this picture of age and gender in small firms, those working past the

Table 13 **The age distribution of employees according to firm size**

	Firm size according to number of employees							
	1–10	11–24	25–49	50–249	DNK but 50–499	250–499	500+	Total
Aged 16–24	805,079	753,053	527,702	694,448	138,045	188,889	393,563	3,500,779
	17.32%	20.32%	15.76%	11.98%	18.19%	10.26%	8.76%	14.23%
Aged 25–39	1,395,294	1,201,335	1,114,449	2,050,340	271,900	644,878	1,782,264	8,460,460
	30.01%	32.42%	33.29%	35.37%	35.83%	35.03%	39.65%	34.40%
Aged 40–49	1,106,672	821,546	840,308	1,550,601	176,590	518,129	1,247,686	6,261,532
	23.81%	22.17%	25.10%	26.75%	23.27%	28.14%	27.76%	25.46%
Aged 50–64	1,190,745	848,349	805,244	1,414,754	160,467	469,766	1,024,128	5,913,453
	25.61%	22.89%	24.05%	24.41%	21.15%	25.52%	22.78%	24.04%
Aged 65+	151,106	81,339	60,276	86,802	11,771	19,376	47,431	458,101
	3.25%	2.20%	1.80%	1.50%	1.55%	1.05%	1.06%	1.86%
Total	4,648,896	3,705,622	3,347,979	5,796,945	758,773	1,841,038	4,495,072	24,594,325

Source: Quarterly *Labour Force Survey*, April–June 2009. DNK = do not know.

age of 65 are particularly likely to be self-employed. Similarly, splitting each of the gender-age groups in Table 1 into those with, and those without, dependants aged 16 or less, we find that self-employment is much more prevalent among those with children. For instance, among men aged between 40 and 49, those with dependants under 17 years of age have a 19 per cent rate of self-employment, compared with only 15 per cent among those without (LFS, 2009). The figures for women of the same age group are 11 per cent and 7 per cent respectively. These findings are confirmed by multivariate studies (Brown et al., 2007) and we cannot rule out the possibility that similar considerations may be driving the findings in Table 13.

The implication from Tables 12 and 13 is that, the larger the firm, the less likely we are to observe women and older or younger workers among employees. The fact that age and sex discrimination legislation were introduced in response to suggestions that these groups were experiencing forms of discrimination in the labour market may imply some potential role for small businesses in providing employment opportunities to disadvantaged groups. We have also seen, however, that many more factors could be at work here, and therefore need to look more closely at other aspects of disadvantage.

Table 14 begins by considering the distribution of the highest educational qualifications among the employees of firms of different sizes. Those who achieve degree level or higher qualifications are particularly concentrated among the largest firms, with 38 per cent of employees in large firms reporting that they have achieved this level of qualification – in contrast, only 17 per cent of employees in micro-businesses have done so. When we consider individuals whose highest level of qualification is anything other than degree and HNC/HND, however, we are more likely to find higher proportions in smaller firms. The pattern is not always uniform, possibly because in some cases we experience problems with sample size, but given also the fact that 10.7 per cent of employees in micro-businesses have no qualifications, compared with only 3.8 per cent in the largest firms, it would seem clear that opportunities for employment of the less well qualified (and those with vocational qualifications) are much more concentrated among small firms.

Following the lead given in the previous section of this chapter, Table 15 presents evidence on the extent to which we observe employees who report language difficulties within firms of different sizes. It is important to remember that the employees included in Table 15 are those who report 'other' as the language spoken at home. Comparing the proportions of this 'other' group with those who report speaking English or Celtic languages at home across firms of different sizes suggests no particular pattern. We can see from Table 15, however, that those who report facing some form of disadvantage (in this case, problems of obtaining or keeping a job) are much more likely to make up a larger proportion of workers in the smaller firms.

Table 16 presents evidence on the extent to which we observe those who report different categories of economic activity twelve months previously, in firms of different sizes now. As one might expect with such a fine distinction of previous and present economic activity status, some of the cells are poorly populated and therefore we are forced to merge categories. Once again, however, the pattern here suggests that those who are working now, but were unemployed or in some other way outside the labour market twelve months ago, are more likely to be working in small rather than large firms.

Table 14 **The distribution of employees according to highest qualification by firm size**

| | Firm size according number of employees | | |
	1–10	11–24	25–49
Degree, higher or equivalent	752,401 16.18%	666,227 17.98%	723,661 21.61%
HNC, HND, BTEC, etc. Higher	294,534 6.34%	240,322 6.49%	226,608 6.77%
ONC, OND, BTEC, etc. National	84,405 1.82%	68,164 1.84%	72,977 2.18%
C&G, RSA, Diploma, NVQ3	542,193 11.66%	455,730 12.3%	392,574 11.73%
A-level and equivalent	334,447 7.19%	285,883 7.71%	219,317 6.55%
Trade apprenticeship	227,860 4.9%	143,769 3.88%	156,439 4.67%
O-level and equiv. GCSE A–C	896,764 19.29%	664,699 17.94%	566,262 16.91%
NVQ level 2 or equivalent	297,114 6.39%	263,795 7.12%	240,462 7.18%
CSE below grade 1 and vocational equivalent	219,759 4.73%	169,316 4.57%	141,387 4.22%
Other	388,488 8.36%	271,328 7.32%	232,038 6.93%
No qualification	496,815 10.69%	353,211 9.53%	250,031 7.47%
Total*	4,648,896	3,705,622	3,347,979

* Teaching, nursing and do not know (DNK) are not presented for ease of exposition, but are included in total column frequency
Source: Quarterly *Labour Force Survey*, April–June 2009

50–249	DNK but 50–499	250–499	500+	Total
1,657,263	184,596	499,801	1,707,382	6,191,331
28.59%	24.33%	27.15%	37.98%	25.17%
380,689	37,374	132,978	355,632	1,668,137
6.57%	4.93%	7.22%	7.91%	6.78%
100,456	9,114	46,576	80,252	461,944
1.73%	1.2%	2.53%	1.79%	1.88%
577,041	45,792	176,896	391,345	2,581,571
9.95%	6.04%	9.61%	8.71%	10.5%
395,756	54,176	136,888	288,809	1,715,276
6.83%	7.14%	7.44%	6.43%	6.97%
212,434	30,320	73,822	120,008	964,652
3.66%	4.00%	4.01%	2.67%	3.92%
905,437	129,599	296,342	579,199	4,038,302
15.62%	17.08%	16.1%	12.89%	16.42%
346,141	31,265	113,466	199,488	1,491,731
5.97%	4.12%	6.16%	4.44%	6.07%
222,566	45,211	70,602	134,061	1,002,902
3.84%	5.96%	3.83%	2.98%	4.08%
460,265	74,776	137,183	257,223	1,821,301
7.94%	9.85%	7.45%	5.72%	7.41%
377,430	73,017	111,589	172,350	1,834,443
6.51%	9.62%	6.06%	3.83%	7.46%
5,796,945	758,773	1,841,038	4,495,072	24,594,325

Table 15 **Whether employee reports having any difficulty getting/keeping a job (owing to language)**

	Firm size according to number of employees						
	1–10	11–24	25–49	50–249	DNK but 50–499	250–499	500+	Total
Yes, language is a problem	41,187 17.6%	27,223 14.12%	14,142 9.69%	30,283 11.01%	9,090 14.45%	8,055 9.14%	20,566 8.01%	150,546 11.99%
No, language is not a problem	192,781 82.4%	165,587 85.88%	131,865 90.31%	244,707 88.99%	53,810 85.55%	80,094 90.86%	236,168 91.99%	1,105,012 88.01%
Total	233,968	192,810	146,007	274,990	62,900	88,149	256,734	1,255,558

Source: Quarterly *Labour Force Survey*, July–September 2009. DNK = do not know.

Table 16 **Distribution of employees according to main economic activity status twelve months ago**

| | | | Firm size according to number of employees | | | | | |
	1–10	11–24	25–49	50–249	DNK but 50–499	250–499	500+	Total
Working in paid job or business	3,579,023 92.12%	2,815,407 91.53%	2,619,052 93.76%	4,605,993 94.68%	562,252 91.21%	1,506,826 96.88%	3,639,264 96.46%	19,327,817 93.99%
Unemployed or 'not in waged employment'	93,583 2.41%	64,222 2.09%	42,159 1.51%	79,504 1.63%	17,444 2.83%	15,721 1.01%	38,582 1.02%	351,215 1.71%
Full-time student	138,325 3.56%	150,334 4.89%	97,145 3.48%	129,169 2.66%	30,894 5.01%	26,172 1.68%	67,629 1.79%	639,668 3.11%
Looking after family or home; long-term sick or disabled; and retired	74,195 1.91%	45,963 1.49%	34,924 1.25%	50,302 1.03%	5,855 0.95%	6,599 0.42%	27,176 0.72%	245,014 1.19%
Total	3,885,126	3,075,926	2,793,280	4,864,968	616,445	1,555,318	3,772,651	20,563,714

Source: Quarterly *Labour Force Survey*, April–June 2009. DNK = do not know.

There has been very little research in this area, but whatever the debates over push and pull into self-employment (that is, whether disadvantaged groups are pulled in or pushed out) there is evidence that self-employment is more prevalent among disadvantaged groups. Furthermore there is stronger evidence that disadvantaged groups make up a larger proportion of employees in smaller firms.

Some commentators may be tempted to dismiss such findings and suggest that they further question the value of employee jobs in small firms and self-employment. The differences we observe could be due to the fact that smaller firms and the self-employed are more likely to engage in forms of economic activity that are in some ways 'marginal' – they are on the margins of survival, whereas larger firms are more stable and involved in less marginal (higher value-added) activities. This is the essential challenge of Brown et al. (1990), who suggested that (on average) the jobs created in smaller firms do not last as long, are associated with lower wages, lesser terms and conditions and do not involve as much training. Thus, it may be that jobs in smaller firms are (on average) lower-skilled, less secure, etc., and therefore those with fewer opportunities elsewhere in the labour market are more likely to be found in this form of employment.

Brown et al. (ibid.) took their findings to suggest that governments should be more cautious in encouraging small-firm growth. Any concerns that small-firm employees are more vulnerable or exploited do not seem to be borne out, however, as they report higher levels of satisfaction in various aspects of the employment relationship and report statistically significant lower levels of work-related illness (Forth et al., 2006; Urwin et al., 2008a). More importantly, we are not faced with a viable, affordable policy alternative that would generate 'good' employment opportunities for disadvantaged groups. In this situation, suggesting that promotion of small businesses and self-employment should be curtailed implies fewer job opportunities for the disadvantaged.

Reducing the obstacles to self-employment is probably not the most important policy priority. Indeed, the obstacles to setting up a business in the UK are limited. Groups that may struggle in hierarchical and formal labour markets are certainly well represented among the self-employed (though this differs between ethnic groups), but the more convincing evidence relates to the employment of disadvantaged groups among small firms. Removing obstacles to the creation and growth of small businesses would seem to represent one of the main pathways to employment for many disadvantaged groups. Furthermore, as we shall see in Chapter 4, the very process of job creation and destruction that is at the centre of concerns over jobs in small firms is particularly important to the workings of the wider economy.

Multivariate analysis

This section discusses the results of multivariate analysis. To begin with the analysis examined the factors that determine whether somebody is working as an employee; a self-employed person with employees; or self-employed without employees. This is a very similar approach to that taken in Chapter 2, but simply incorporates an additional distinction between the self-employed with and without employees, and also includes some of the factors discussed in this section as additional explanatory variables.

Then the analysis looks at the likelihood of different groups being employees in firms of different sizes. This is achieved using an ordered Probit model which has as its dependent variable firms of different sizes modelled as an ordered scale (i.e. the largest firms are given a value of [7], the next-largest a [6] and so on until we reach the micro-businesses that are coded as [1]). The aim is to determine which, among the many factors we have discussed, are (statistically) significantly associated with working in these different-sized firms (with the analysis limited to firms in the private sector).

It is important to note that, even more than was the case when considering a straightforward employee/self-employed split, these are not causal models – they do not purport to describe *why* firms are different sizes or *why* people take up self-employment of different forms. Rather they simply bring together the considerations of various individual characteristics and allow us to ask questions such as: if we account for the differing levels of part-time employment in firms of different sizes, is it the case that there are no longer any significant differences in the proportions of women and men in different-sized firms? Similarly, when we consider ethnicity, immigration and language there are a lot of potentially overlapping effects and a multivariate analysis allows us to get an overview of what may be more or less closely associated with working as a self-employed person or an employee.

The approach is similar to that taken by Cowling et al. (2004), who use data from the British Household Panel Survey (BHPS) to carry out one of the few existing UK studies of self-employment that differentiates between those with and without employees. One difference in the approach adopted here is that Cowling et al. model a two-stage process. The decision of whether to become self-employed (with or without employees) as opposed to an employee is seen as the first stage in the decision process of economic agents. The second stage is that, once self-employed, individuals decide whether or not to employ staff. The discussions in our first two chapters would suggest that the labour market state of being self-employed without employees is so different from that of being a small business owner-manager (self-employed with employees) that this two-stage process is inappropriate. Furthermore, we already have what may be considered a first-stage selection equation at the end of Chapter 2 and can refer to this for parameter estimates if needed.

Therefore our results simply show the probability that individuals are observed in the two states of self-employment, relative to the state of being an employee. The main findings that are both relevant and statistically significant are:

- It is still the case that, at all levels of educational attainment (both higher and lower), we are less likely to observe somebody as self-employed with or without employees, when compared with those whose highest qualification is A-level.
- Women are no more or less likely to be observed as self-employed without employees, when compared with having an employee job; but they are significantly less likely to be working as self-employed with employees.
- Having dependants aged under sixteen makes one more likely to be in both states of self-employment. If an individual is married or cohabiting, they are significantly more likely to be self-employed with employees; but this makes no difference to the probability that they will be observed as self-employed without employees, relative to being an employee.
- Considering ethnicity, relative to the reference group of white British and other individuals, those who report Indian

as their ethnicity are significantly more likely to be self-employed with employees. They are, however, no more or less likely to be self-employed without employees. In contrast, individuals of Pakistani and Chinese origin are significantly more likely to be in both states of self-employment.

- Interestingly, we find that those who own their properties outright (and so have collateral against which to borrow) are significantly more likely to be self-employed without employees. They are not, however, more likely to be self-employed with employees (though the latter effect could be a result of small cell sizes).

- Those who report that their country of birth is in eastern Europe, North America, Central/South America or central Asia are significantly more likely to be self-employed without employees relative to having an employee job (but there is no effect on the state of self-employment with employees). While those from the Balkans, Russia, the Caucasus and Turkey are significantly more likely to be in both states of self-employment relative to being an employee (something that could be driven by those of Turkish origin in this group). Those from East and South Asia are significantly less likely to be self-employed without employees, relative to having an employee job.

- In comparison with those who report that their religion is Christian, individuals who report being Buddhist, Jewish, Muslim, any other religion and no religion are all significantly more likely to be self-employed without employees, compared with being an employee. Only those of the Jewish faith (and 'any other religion') are significantly more likely than those of the Christian faith to be self-employed with employees.

With regard to the tendency of people to work for small and large firms we find the following:

- Those whose highest qualification is above A-level are significantly more likely to be working in larger firms, while those with no qualifications are significantly more likely to be working in smaller firms. Those with a highest qualification of NVQ level 2 are an interesting exception, as they are also more likely to be working in larger firms.
- Individuals who report having dependants aged under sixteen are significantly less likely to be working in larger firms.
- Individuals of Indian, Other Asian and Black Caribbean origin are significantly more likely to be working in large firms (relative to the reference category of White British and other white). In contrast, those of Chinese descent are significantly less likely to be working as an employee in a large firm.
- It is interesting to note that, relative to the largest group of 'homeowners' (who are buying their house with a mortgage or loan), those whom we might consider as more advantaged (those owning their home outright) and those who may be relatively disadvantaged (i.e. they are in some form of rental accommodation) are significantly less likely to be observed in large firms.
- Relative to those who twelve months ago were in waged employment, those who were unemployed, long-term sick or disabled, looking after the family home, retired or a student are significantly more likely to be in smaller firms.
- Relative to those who report being of the Christian faith, individuals who are Buddhist, Jewish, Muslim or Sikh are significantly more likely to be working in smaller firms.

Conclusion

Small firms have particular characteristics which lead them to employ those who are otherwise disadvantaged within the hierarchical labour markets of large firms. It is also the case that many of those groups have a tendency to be self-employed. The disadvantage of such groups when it comes to employment opportunities with larger firms may arise as a result of natural information asymmetries within the market for labour. Alternatively, it may arise as a result of the disproportionate effect that employment legislation has on those without formal qualifications, formal work histories and so on, because they cannot 'signal' their qualities to employers. Self-employment is clearly a way of overcoming such problems – especially as employment protection legislation is irrelevant to the self-employed. Small firms may also have the opportunity to be more flexible in their hiring practices and may be able to acquire information about those who have few formal qualifications, lack language skills and so on – especially if the firms are employing other family members. The following facts are especially pertinent:

- Self-employment accounts for nearly 20 per cent of males who are active in the labour market.
- Self-employment is especially important for groups that might value flexibility in their working arrangements. It accounts, for example, for 42 per cent of males who are active in the labour market and aged over 65.
- Self-employment is also important for certain ethnic groups, those who have been sick and disabled and those for whom English is not their first language.
- Small firms tend to employ more part-time workers, more

women, more older people, more people who regard English as a barrier to employment and more poorly educated people.

- There is, however, no obvious impediment to self-employment. Indeed, self-employment may be high in some groups because of the impediments to formal employment and to the self-employed taking on employees. On balance, there are also probably no strong artificial benefits from being self-employed. While there are tax advantages, there are compliance costs and various National Insurance benefits are not received by the self-employed.
- Consistent with the argument that small firms are suffering impediments to growth of employment is the fact that, while self-employment without employees has grown, the very smallest firms in the 'micro-enterprise' category were squeezed between 2000 and 2009.
- Studies suggest that starting a business in the UK is easy but that there are many restrictions on growth and taking on new employees. This leads to less enterprise in general but also fewer employment opportunities for particular vulnerable groups, and might lead people to be pushed into self-employment.

This analysis will help inform the policy conclusions in Chapter 6.

4 BUSINESS BIRTHS AND FAILED EXPERIMENTS

We have seen how self-employment can act as a potential labour supply route for those who face problems securing an employee job. Furthermore, when comparing the characteristics of employees in small and large firms, we observe a larger proportion of potentially disadvantaged individuals among the former. Self-employment and the jobs that the self-employed (small business owner-managers) create seem to offer opportunities to many individuals who face barriers when attempting to secure an employee job.

If we consider once again that the size of a firm is a 'proxy' for self-employment (with self-employed owner-managers more likely to predominate among smaller firms), 31 per cent of UK employment in 2009 was in enterprises that had between 1 and 49 employees; compared with 12 per cent among firms with 50 to 249 employees and 40 per cent in firms larger than this.[1] From our study of the 2009 LFS and BERR statistics it would appear that there are approximately four million businesses run by the self-employed at any one point in time. Taken together these figures give some idea of the contribution to employment of the self-employed without employees and small-business owner-managers.

---

1   Enterprise Directorate Analytical Unit at BIS.

This static picture of employment shares, however, hides an underlying dynamic of continual job creation and destruction. Just over half of new businesses are not in existence five years on from their birth. These high rates of firm 'churn' make jobs in larger (usually older) establishments more secure than those in younger (usually smaller) firms, and this has pushed many commentators to question the value of the jobs created by smaller firms (see, for instance, Brown et al., 1990). In contrast, for many academics this high rate of small-firm churn is essential to the role that new entrants play in the process of creative destruction (see, for instance, Schumpeter, 1934, 1989; OECD, 2004), which creates the large successful firms of the future. In other words, it is not that there is anything naturally 'second-rate' about small-firm jobs; their insecurity is a natural part of the entrepreneurial process without which no big firms would ever be created.

In this chapter we first consider the findings from research that attempts to capture some of the detail from this dynamic environment of creation and destruction. The debate on rates of job creation and destruction across small and large firms has been raging since the early 1980s, and we bring this up to date with a consideration of the research into high-growth firms. Having mapped out the 'demography' of business births and deaths, we then consider the role that the self-employed with and without employees are likely to play in this process.

Births, deaths and marriages

The question of which size firms contribute most to job creation has its roots in the work of David Birch (1979, 1981 and 1987), whose studies of the USA suggested that between 1969 and 1976, 66 per cent of all net new jobs could be attributed to firms with twenty or fewer employees. Among the large number of studies that followed on from Birch's work, some have provided confirmation and others have challenged the suggestion that smaller firms predominate in the process of net job creation (for a good review, see Neumark et al., 2008) ('NWZ').

Part of the debate has focused on the evidence that smaller firms create more jobs, but also destroy more in any given time interval than larger firms, and thus the net job-creation picture hides much more volatile gross worker flows. For instance, in their study of UK manufacturing, Barnes and Haskel (2002a) suggest that, during the 1980s, establishments with fewer than one hundred employees accounted for approximately 41 per cent of jobs destroyed and somewhere between 59 per cent and 63 per cent of jobs created.[2]

This still suggests a net contribution that implies that smaller firms are growing and larger firms declining along the lines of the 'trees of the forest' analogy of industrial structure. This finding was corroborated in many studies following on from Birch that continued to identify a disproportionate net contribution to employment from small firms.[3] A more comprehensive challenge to the findings of Birch, however, was provided by Davis et al. (1996a, 1996b) ('DHS'), who suggested that measurement error

---

[2] These are midpoints of the actual figures that Barnes and Haskel arrive at using different methods of calculation, and it should be remembered that, in line with many other studies, the focus of their analysis is manufacturing establishments.

[3] We do not consider here the additional arguments over whether jobs in small and large firms are comparable according to other characteristics (Brown et al., 1990). As we can see from the analysis in Chapter 3, both the type of employment and the individuals employed are different in firms of different sizes.

could explain away many of Birch's findings. The main tenet of the argument of DHS rests on the concept of *regression to the mean*, which has applications across many studies of economic data (Friedman, 1992).

The argument can be put as follows. When we compare the employment growth rates of small and large firms, we must first categorise them as being either small or large according to the number of employees they have at the start of our period of analysis. It is inevitable that some firms categorised as 'small' will be in this category only because of a transitory negative shock or measurement error. In our subsequent periods of measurement, these firms will be seen to experience artificially high growth rates, simply because they were wrongly categorised as small firms (and are now reverting back to their usual levels of employment). The opposite argument holds for firms that are incorrectly categorised as large (owing to measurement error and/or transitory positive shocks) and which subsequently *revert back to their normal* lower levels of employment.

The findings of DHS challenged those of Birch and initiated another round of studies in various countries. This was not only in response to the challenge presented by the potential fallacy of regression to the mean, but also because the work of DHS focused solely on US manufacturing firms. Subsequent studies, however, have still tended to side with the original findings of Birch, even when regression to the mean is accounted for (see NWZ for a good review).

More importantly, two recent studies by NWZ and Halti-wanger et al. (2010) (HJM) using US data provide a possible explanation for contrasting evidence in previous studies and underline the importance of new firms or start-ups in the process of job creation. Both papers undertake a rigorous and detailed investigation which attempts to overcome many of the methodological challenges posed in previous work. While only HJM model the age of the firm explicitly (using the Census Bureau Longitudinal Business Database), the findings of both papers would seem to underline the importance of new business start-ups.

Thus, using US National Establishment Time Series data from 1992 to 2004, NWZ first suggest that the smallest firms (of fewer than twenty workers) have disproportionately high rates of job creation (relative to their total employment share), but also have disproportionately large job-destruction rates. They experience some variation in findings when altering methods in line with DHS, but 'qualitatively' the finding remains of a larger net contribution to new job creation for these smallest of firms. When they remove firm births from the data, however, and focus solely on 'ongoing' firms, much of the relationship between size and job creation disappears. This finding would seem to be supported by HJM, who control for firm age explicitly in their modelling of employment creation and destruction across firms of different sizes. Their findings suggest that, once one accounts for firm age, any firm-size/job-creation relationship disappears. HJM also find, however, that the importance of firm age in explaining job-creation rates is primarily driven by the higher rates of creation and destruction among the youngest (i.e. new) business start-ups.

These new studies imply that previous findings on the relationship between firm size and employment generation are driven by firm age and, more accurately, the important role of new entrants in net employment generation. In the consideration of their findings, HJM (p. 25) suggest they support:

a rich 'up or out' dynamic of startups and young firms that
is consistent with models of market selection and learning ...
after five years about 40 percent of the jobs initially created
by startups have been eliminated by exit ... [but] conditional
on survival, young firms grow more rapidly than their more
mature counterparts.

At first one may view the increased interest in *high-growth firms*
in the UK as a focus on the 'up' firms in the 'up or out' dynamic of
HJM. Thus, while much of the mainstream work on job creation
and destruction considers aggregate impacts of firms grouped
by size, age, sector and other categories, the literature attempts
to identify ongoing firms that account for a disproportionate
share of employment creation. For instance, a report by Stangler
(2010) on the publicly available aspects of the US data studied by
HJM suggests that approximately 40 per cent of all new jobs are
created by the top 1 per cent of fastest-growing firms and that a
few 'gazelles' (variously defined: see Henrekson and Johansson,
2010) are particularly important in this. Once again, however, the
dynamic nature of this environment is underlined, as the smaller,
high-growth firms are still prone to high rates of destruction and
very few of them become large incumbent 'scale' firms.

In the UK, the National Endowment for Science, Technology
and the Arts (NESTA) commissioned research into high-growth
firms using UK data on job creation and destruction between 2005
and 2008 (Anyadike-Danes et al., 2009). The suggestion from the
research is that only 6 per cent of ongoing firms with ten or more
employees can be considered as 'high-growth', and that this 6 per
cent accounted for more than half of new jobs over the period
considered. Unfortunately, the methods adopted in the NESTA
report differ from those used in the job-creation and destruction

literature, and this makes comparison problematic. Most notable is the fact that, within the NESTA report, high-growth firms are defined as those with a minimum of ten employees at the start of the period of analysis, which experience, on average, annual growth rates above 20 per cent over a three-year period. In adopting these criteria the NESTA report is following Eurostat and OECD conventions,[4] but in doing so it would seem that they aim to identify a very specific type of 'high-growth' firm (HGF), which may not be particularly consistent with the 'up' of HJM.

More specifically, the criteria adopted in the NESTA work identify firms that exhibit *consistently* high growth rates over three years, rather than the top given percentage of firms that show the highest growth rates over a one- or two-year period. Thus, while we can view the NESTA study as a search for *some* of the 'up' firms in the 'up or out' environment, the use of rigid criteria is likely only to identify a certain subset of (relatively stable) high-growth firms. As Daunfeldt et al. (2010) suggest, 'HGFs of different definitions are usually not the same firms', and the evidence from a

4   While the convention is one followed in OECD publications (see, for instance, Ahmad, 2006), p. 61 of the Eurostat-OECD *Manual on Business Demography Statistics* (2007) makes only a passing reference to the work of DHS and the measures they adopt. Furthermore, there is little rationale for the adoption of the high-growth firm measure used in the NESTA report other than that it is 'Perhaps the simplest type of indicator …, and moreover one that has clearer interpretability'. This seems to be a questionable assertion given that it is harder to compare with existing evidence and there is no discussion of the many challenges faced by those researching in this area (see NWZ and HJM). For instance, cutting off at ten employees gives problems of regression to the mean and is likely to downplay growth at the bottom end of the age/size distribution; the reason for not including zero-age firms (new starts) is mainly consideration of turnover and not employment growth, and generally there is a departure from the approach of existing researchers, who worry about using categorical cut-off points because of the biases they may introduce.

review carried out by Delmar et al. (2003) suggests extensive variation in the measures used.

We can get a taste for the type of firms that the NESTA work has identified by considering evidence from some follow-up work in Scotland, which suggests that high-growth firms identified using these criteria were more likely to have been 'pre-incubated' in some way, either as part of another business entity or as part of a management/employee buyout (Mason, 2011). The implication is that these firms, because of previous stable performance, were considered to be a good marriage proposition.

Finally, the findings of the NESTA study identify Wales, Northern Ireland, Scotland and the North-East as having higher shares of high-growth firms in the local economy than other parts of the country. When we look at the (percentage) rates of business birth for these parts of the UK over the period of the study, we can see that they do exhibit higher-than-average rates of business start-up (Office for National Statistics, 2010). They are also the four areas of the country with the lowest numbers of active, ongoing businesses, however, and each one accounts for a lower proportion of businesses than its share of the population would suggest.[5] There must also be some concern over the usefulness of a measure of high-growth firms that has the USA with a lower proportion of high-growth firms than the UK.

---

5   For instance, the North-East accounts for 5 per cent of the UK population, but only 2.7 per cent of ongoing businesses; while Scotland has 8.4 per cent of the population, but only 6.4 per cent of ongoing businesses (LFS, April–June 2009, and ONS Business Demography, 2009).

Can we predict success a priori?

There are clearly some interesting findings coming out of the research that attempts to map the demography of firms. Large numbers of firms are starting up all the time and they seem to be responsible for a substantial proportion of gross job creation at any one point in time; while they also destroy many more jobs than ongoing firms (many start-ups are very short-lived), they seem to produce net job creation. Furthermore, out of this ferment of activity, a very small number of firms move up the size and age distribution and, while they are doing so, they account for a large proportion of employment generation.

While useful, these findings are relatively descriptive and provide little insight into what drives success and failure within firms. There is likely to be an important role for industry structure (Klepper and Graddy, 1990) in determining the proportion of high-growth firms, as one would expect the number of firms to be growing in infant industries and flattening off thereafter. Similarly, the existing literature underlines how firm size and survival rates are likely to vary according to factors such as the fixed costs of entering an industry and the existence of economies of scale (for a good review, see Audretsch et al., 2004).

This lack of evidence on causality reflects the relative paucity of appropriate firm- or establishment-level data, when compared with the multitude of micro-data that have the individual or household as the unit of assessment. More importantly, we must ask how far such analyses can progress our understanding if they do not have the potential for insight into the role played by individuals in starting and running these firms.

Research has provided some indication of the numbers flowing through different stages of the UK entrepreneurial 'pipeline'. On average we can expect in the region of 270,000 firms to be starting up in any one year (with some rise during recessions). At the end of five years, just under half (46.8 per cent) of these remain (ONS Business Demography statistics). Of those that do not make it through these first five years, there are two main outcomes. The first is business death, where the firm is no longer in operation, because it is either not making a sufficient return to justify its continued existence and/or the owner-manager gets a better (perhaps employee job) offer. We can expect individuals in this instance to either remain in alternative states of the labour market (unemployed, employee or inactive) or return to self-employment to start up a new entity, with or without a break in between.

Using existing data it is difficult to find what proportion of the 270,000 who start businesses in any given year are serial entrepreneurs. Similarly, there are problems identifying those firms that are reborn as another entity, perhaps as part of a merger, buyout or simply a legal change of name and company number. In the US studies considered in the previous section, indicators have been created in the data to flag when a new firm is not a wholly new entity (and BIS are undertaking the same process). This still does not help in identifying whether a firm has become a new entity because it was failing or prospering, however, and, again, we have no information on the individual entrepreneurs involved in this process.

Of the approximately 130,000 firms surviving after five years, the majority will stay small, perhaps employing a few workers, but with no desire (or ability) to grow beyond a certain size. There are few clear estimates of the proportion of these 130,000 surviving firms which go on to become the large-scale firms of the future. At any one time, however, there are fewer than 6,000 private sector businesses in the UK employing 250 or more employees.[6] If we assume that 5 per cent of these large firms are being replaced each year, then there is perhaps a one-in-a-thousand chance that a start-up will become a large-scale firm of the future. When we consider what little information the firm-level data contains, this is quite a modelling challenge. Indeed, the only thing that would seem certain is the quote from Marshall:

> The young trees of the forest struggle upwards through the benumbing shade of their older rivals. Many succumb on the way, and a few only survive; those few become stronger with every year, they get a large share of light and air with every increase of their height. (Marshall, 1949 [1920])

Daunfeldt et al. (2010) suggest that whatever measures we use, high-growth firms are more likely to be younger firms but not necessarily the very youngest firms started up within the last year. The group of high-growth firms changes constantly, as we experience high levels of attrition. As such, identifying a group of firms that is growing rapidly at one time and that will continue to grow is more or less impossible. Furthermore, the high-growth firms are likely to be a heterogeneous group. This means that using a public policy approach to incubate and pick winners is more or less impossible. The research in this field about the nature of start-ups and growing firms confirms the Austrian School understanding of entrepreneurship. Stangler (2010) suggests that 'policies aimed at somehow making companies of the high-growth variety will necessarily be a blunt and static instrument acting on a dynamic target'.

---

6   BIS, *SME Statistics for the UK and Regions*, 2009.

There would seem to be an implicit search for stability and order in the approach of those attempting to identify 'high-growth' firms, and this seems particularly evident when we consider many of the policy recommendations arising from these studies. For instance, Anyadike-Danes et al. (2009: 5) suggest that 'merely encouraging start-ups is unlikely to lead to dramatic growth if they fail to expand. Policymakers should focus on quality and not just quantity.' In a similar vein, Shane (2009) questions the wisdom of wholesale support for start-ups and suggests that policymakers should 'encourage high quality, high growth companies to be founded'.

Comparing this to quotes from US researchers working in the same field, we get an idea of the divergence of views across the Atlantic that arise from very similar research findings. For instance, HJM (p. 25) suggest: 'findings help interpret the popular perception of the role of small businesses as job creators in a manner that is consistent with theories that highlight the role of business formation, experimentation, selection and learning as important features of the U.S. economy'. US researchers place a value on *experimentation, selection and learning*. The UK researchers seem to consider many failures to be a 'waste of scarce resources' (Parker, 2004: 229) and suggest that one can obtain success with less 'waste' by picking the right sort of firms to support.

Are these two differing views on how best to nurture innovation, entrepreneurship and ultimately growth diametrically opposed? In the case of the US researchers there would seem to be an implicit assumption that a 'failed experiment' has value, as it adds to knowledge and understanding, and ultimately successful experiments are built on the back of what we discover from failed experiments. Furthermore, there is an inevitable risk in entrepreneurial ventures – the market process needs to select the successful ventures and it is not possible to select in advance those ventures that will succeed.

We have seen how analysis of firm- and establishment-level data produces generally descriptive findings, owing partly to the fact that much of the potential for a causal analysis would require us to consider the characteristics of the individual (or entrepreneur). So the question is whether the findings using individual-level data allow us to predict success with a high degree of accuracy. One of the most comprehensive reviews of the evidence on what drives success and failure in self-employment and entrepreneurship is that of Parker (2004). The following summarises some of the areas where (pp. 222–5) there is evidence of (statistically) significant 'determinants of survival in self-employment (for individuals) and business (for firms) in developed countries'.[7]

1. Human capital
a) Previous experience of self-employment has a positive impact on the chance of survival in any present employment spell (while previous managerial experience is not found to have an impact). More generally, Cowling et al. (2004) suggest that 'job-related human capital' has more importance than formally accredited academic qualifications.
b) The suggestion is that *Skilled Manual* and *Professional* occupations have lower probabilities of exit (citing the work of Taylor, 1999).
c) As one would perhaps expect, there is a suggestion that exit to bankruptcy is less likely for the more highly qualified, while

7   Here we highlight the factors that represent an addition to our discussions to date.

exit to alternative employment is more likely (especially in a boom).

2. The middle-aged seem to have higher survival rates (when compared with both younger and older people).
3. Those with higher levels of finance at start-up (which is not in the form of debt financing) seem to do better.
4. Ownership structure, such as franchises, may have an impact on success.

Most well-informed lay persons could perhaps have guessed these drivers of success and failure. Furthermore, Parker suggests in his conclusion that academic researchers have achieved only limited success in identifying the factors that are conducive to business survival and growth (p. 228).

One interesting aspect of the evidence presented by Parker, however, is the issue of serial entrepreneurship – as previous experience of self-employment seems to have more bearing on success than academic qualifications. As suggested in earlier chapters, the nature of the self-employment choice needs to be seen as a repeated game (or lottery), and according to some key theories (Jovanovic, 1982) the only way for an individual to find out about their entrepreneurial ability is to attempt self-employment. If entrepreneurs learn 'on the job' then perhaps some of these 'doomed-to-failure' ventures serve as learning experiences for those who subsequently become successful.

Similarly, the poor performance of econometric models at the individual level is perhaps not surprising, given the dynamism of the situation, but also the heterogeneity among those who take up self-employment.

Serial entrepreneurs and the self-employed with or without employees

We are not the first to suggest that the self-employed with and without employees should be studied as separate entities (Cowling et al., 2004). In Chapter 3 we reported the results of a model that added to the insights provided by previous studies. In both our own model and those of previous researchers, however, the approach is static in nature and we are not able to observe transitions between the two states. Cowling et al. suggest that their inclusion of various measures of human capital allows for 'learning-by-doing', but there is still no explicit modelling of transitions. While evidence of differences between the two groups is of interest, it does not answer the question of what role (if any) the self-employed without employees play in the process of employment generation.

Consider Table 17, reproduced from Anyadike-Danes et al. (2009: 36), which describes the employment situation in 2008 of an original cohort of 221,731 firms 'born' in 1998. Unfortunately the focus of the table is on all firms that have at least one employee at the start of the period of analysis, so we are likely to rule out many of the self-employed without employees (see the discussion in Chapter 2). Nevertheless, it still gives us some indication of the employment generation potential of the smallest enterprises. The table is based on the 643,000 jobs, as of 2008, in firms that have survived from the original 1998 cohort. Looking across the first row of the table we can see that by 2008 16 per cent of all the employment in firms of twenty-plus employees is in those firms that started off with one employee recorded. Furthermore, while 58 per cent of firms starting with a single employee still had only one employee at the end of the period, 25.5 per cent of all employment in firms that were born in 1998 was in firms that had one employee in 1998. The vast majority of these employees (84 per cent) were employed by firms that had expanded their employee base over the ten-year period.

Table 17 **Employment of firms surviving in 2008, from the cohort of 1998 start-ups (origin/destination matrix by size-band, %)**

		Destination size-band, 2008							
		1	2	3	4	5–9	10–19	20+	All
Origin size-band, 1998	1	4.0	2.7	1.3	1.3	3.4	2.7	10.0	25.5
	2	0.9	1.7	0.7	0.7	1.9	1.6	3.0	10.5
	3	0.2	0.5	0.5	0.4	1.2	1.0	2.2	6.0
	4	0.1	0.2	0.2	0.3	0.9	0.9	2.2	4.8
	5–9	0.2	0.2	0.3	0.4	1.8	2.0	7.2	12.0
	10–19	0.1	0.1	0.1	0.1	0.6	1.5	9.4	11.7
	20+	0.0	0.0	0.0	0.0	0.2	0.5	28.7	29.5
	All	5.5	5.4	3.0	3.2	9.9	10.2	62.7	100.0

Source: ONS Business Structure Database, Anyadike-Danes et al. (2009)
Table reproduced with permission

It is more difficult to find evidence that being self-employed without employees acts as a training ground for those who subsequently become self-employed with employees. As the data from HJM implies, many entities seem to come into existence with a large number of employees and, while there is a range of potential explanations for this, we cannot rule out the fact that serial entrepreneurs are key in this respect. Indeed, previous entrepreneurial experience – in contrast to management experience – is a determinant of present entrepreneurial success (Parker, 2004) and some of the most recognised theoretical models consider initial periods of self-employment as processes of learning and testing of ability (see, for instance, Jovanovic, 1982; Frank, 1998). Though the study of serial entrepreneurs is a growing area of research (see Blackburn and Kovalainen, 2009), it has yet to provide insights into the start-up process, as the focus of study is often ongoing firms (see, for instance, Westhead et al., 2005).

Regulation and legislation

In Chapter 2 we considered how the tax system, regulation and legislation seem to incentivise self-employment without employees, but also discourage the taking on of employees by small business owners. We have now seen how dynamic the process of job creation and destruction is, as well as touching on one of the major policy fault-lines – that is, the value that we place on firm failure. In the light of these insights, we now revisit some of the evidence and debates on the impacts of legislation and regulation.

Unfortunately, when considering much of the evidence on how legislation and regulation have an impact on small businesses (in the context of the job creation and destruction dynamics previously described), the most striking features are the shortcomings of the methods used. For instance, a report commissioned by the Federation of Small Businesses (Urwin et al., 2008a) underlines how much of the research into the impact of regulation asks questions directly of those running small businesses. The questions being asked are (either explicitly or implicitly): does regulation either (i) stop small firms from growing or (ii) lead to more firms going out of business? The FSB report details a number of flaws with these studies, including the fact that the phrasing of the questions, and the extent of any descriptions or prompts that describe exactly what is meant by regulation, are likely to influence responses. In addition, there is concern that many business owners simply do not have the same conceptual understandings as the researchers carrying out these studies.[8]

The most serious methodological concern, however, is that these questions are invariably asked of small firms that are, by definition, surviving under the regulatory 'burden'. Ideally one would gauge the extent of any costs of regulation on various firms at a particular point in time and then revisit these firms (setting up what is referred to as a *panel dataset*) to gauge the extent to which they had grown, retained their scale of operation or ceased trading. None of the studies reviewed include small business owners that had ceased trading. It is also the case that many of the studies of the impact of regulation on small businesses are carried out on a population of firms that constitute the membership of employer representative groups. These members often receive legal advice on regulatory compliance as part of the benefits of membership and are a self-selected group of surviving firms. As a result they are not likely to reflect the population of small businesses in the UK.

Given these limitations, policymakers should discard evidence on the impact of regulation that relies on direct questioning of unrepresentative samples of surviving businesses. As there are serious methodological challenges faced by those who attempt to identify a clear impact of regulation and legislation on the prospects of small firms, it is useful to turn to estimates of the relative burden borne by small and large firms. Here there would seem

---

8   For instance, HMRC estimates suggest that only a third of small businesses correctly apply all aspects of maternity legislation (Urwin et al., 2008a) and we can therefore question whether many are actually aware of the full range of regulation and legislation that applies to them.

to be an unavoidable rationale that small firms bear a disproportionate burden of regulation, legislation and tax compliance because it is, to a large extent, a fixed cost. Estimates of the extent of this burden would seem to further suggest that failure to find evidence of an impact is due simply to inappropriate method or a lack of appropriate data.

The essential argument is that the costs of compliance (with respect to firm size) are regressive, as there are economies of scale in tax compliance (Chittenden et al., 2010), as well as fixed costs of complying with product market regulation and employment protection legislation (see, for instance, Urwin et al., 2008a). Considering the costs of complying with the tax system, Chittenden et al. (2010) estimate that: '[they] weigh sixteen times more heavily on the smallest firms than on the largest' and that 'this is a barrier to entrepreneurship, to small-firm formation and to competition'. Worryingly, their study suggests that, while there have been numerous attempts to reduce red tape in the UK, the costs of compliance have remained roughly constant, as any improvements have tended to be offset by changes elsewhere in the system. The authors underline that because costs are disproportionately high for small firms, the implied cost savings of any reductions in red tape can be similarly disproportionately large.

This argument has been used by those representing small businesses to call for less regulation, the repeal of legislation and/or specific exemptions for small businesses. As we have already suggested, however, while the burden of legislation, regulation and taxation may hinder the growth and survival of ongoing small firms (particularly in the context of hiring new staff), these same structures serve to incentivise the use of self-employment, particularly incorporation as a limited company with no employees, over employee relationships. Thus, it can be argued that start-ups are already 'favoured' to some extent within the present system – the concern is that this incentive is taken up by many who are attempting to reduce their compliance burdens, rather than the entrepreneurs that government would wish to encourage. It is the obstacles to the expansion of start-ups which are the problem. We return to these debates and the implications they have for policy in the concluding chapter.

Regarding an expansion of employment protection legislation, the suggestion is that it might cause a fall in the rates of both job creation and destruction in ongoing firms. We would expect employers to be discouraged from creating jobs because of the increased costs associated with such regulation, but this would also provide protection for the jobs of those in employment (see, for instance, van Stel and Stunnenburg, 2004, for a more detailed discussion).

Both higher levels of employment regulation and higher rates of income taxation relative to corporate taxation provide an incentive for people to become self-employed without employees. Such incentives are not economically sound reasons for people starting new firms. They may lead more small business ventures to be doomed to failure, not as part of the process of creative destruction within the marketplace but because people are establishing as self-employed for the wrong reasons.

Conclusion

The evidence presented in this chapter suggests strongly that the growth of new firms is a crucial component of employment growth. Often, though not always, these will be new firms that start life as very small firms. Young firms grow more rapidly and create and destroy more jobs than older firms. This jobs creation arises from a relatively small group within the new firm and small firm sector. In the UK, just 6 per cent of firms create over half of all new jobs, and there is only a one-in-a-thousand chance that a new firm will become a large firm. Furthermore, it is impossible to predict which firms will become successful. Although serial entrepreneurs are more likely to successfully set up growing firms, we know very little else even about the characteristics of successful firms that would allow us to determine, a priori, which ones are even *most likely* to succeed. Generalised support for start-ups will also lead to very many failed ventures being supported.

From this evidence, we can deduce that the most effective way of ensuring that economic growth and job creation arise from the business sector is simply to make sure that the general conditions exist for businesses to flourish. Picking winners is a nonstarter; education and training will also not help, though policies in this area may be oriented towards other goals. Regulation does bear most heavily on small businesses, however, and may therefore inhibit job creation and the flourishing of potentially highly successful firms. Furthermore, there may be other areas (for example, the removal of impediments to accessing finance) in which there is a legitimate policy interest. The evidence that regulation especially impedes small businesses is very important. There is not simply a static cost of such regulation (fewer small firms and higher costs of doing business) but also an unquantifiable dynamic cost in that businesses which might otherwise become large might never go beyond the stage of 'self-employment without employees' as a result of the costs of regulation.

5 SELF-EMPLOYMENT AND ENTREPRENEURIAL INSIGHT

The evidence suggests that there are clearly questions over the extent to which we can predict the 'high-growth' firms of the future. Indeed, the nature of entrepreneurship is such that it often necessitates the prediction of individuals and/or individual firms and is therefore not a goal that is suitable for empirical methods. Similarly, empirical studies to date do not allow us to determine *how important* it is to have an unshackled process of small firm 'experimentation' if we wish to produce 'high-growth' firms and these paradigm-shifting entrepreneurs.

The entrepreneur has been central to the writings of many great thinkers, such as Schumpeter (1934, 1937, 1989), Mises (1949) and Knight (1921). Many of today's most well-known economists, such as Paul Romer and Edmund Phelps (Economist, 2009), consider the entrepreneur and the skills they bring to the economy as central to the process of economic advancement. This chapter examines entrepreneurship by using as building blocks various strands of economic theory to construct a picture of what we actually mean by entrepreneurship; how it relates to the creation of the firm; how it contrasts with self-employment; and what role self-employment might play in supplying entrepreneurial insights to the economy.

Entrepreneurship

Jean-Baptiste Say was one of the first academics to consider the group of economic agents who, as 'entrepreneurs', 'shift economic resources out of an area of lower and into an area of higher productivity and greater yield' (see, for instance, Say, 1803, as quoted in Drucker, 2007). It is the Austrian School, however, which has the entrepreneur as the central component of a business economy. Hayek was one of the first to consider the *process* of competition, as opposed to a Walrasian set of conditions that describe the end point (i.e. equilibrium). As Peter Klein puts it: 'Hayek's notion [is] of an economy characterized by dispersed, tacit knowledge, an economy in which "competition" is a process of coordination and equilibration'.[1] In this there would seem to be a clear role for the entrepreneur, but it is Mises (1949) who explicitly suggests that the 'equilibrating properties of the market process depend vitally upon the activities of entrepreneurs' (as cited in Harper, 2003).

The entrepreneur discovers opportunities in markets such as opportunities to produce products at lower costs, or products of greater value to consumers, and obtains profit from exploiting such opportunities. This is in contrast to the neoclassical paradigm where there really is little room for the entrepreneur (ibid.) – if markets are assumed to be in equilibrium, with all economic actors possessing all relevant information, we have no role for an entrepreneur to add value by discovering more efficient uses of resources (for more detail, see Huerta de Soto, 2008).

This perspective provides a first step in clarifying the difference between the 'entrepreneurial input' and the self-employed. More specifically, we can discern three sets of skills and aptitudes

1   http://austrianeconomists.typepad.com/weblog/2007/11/klein-on-hayek-.html.

that the self-employed/entrepreneur would seem to require. These are (i) the ability to identify entrepreneurial/business opportunities for profit; (ii) a willingness to take on the risks associated with the pursuit of business ideas; and (iii) the ability to manage and direct a business venture.[2]

While there are some potential overlaps, these aspects are essentially distinct. For example, when considering theories of the firm and their management expounded originally by Ronald Coase (1937) and Chester Barnard (lectures from 1938, as reported in Williamson, 2005), the skills required to run the firm are predominantly administrative and cooperative – emphasising managerial/organisational ability. In contrast, the entrepreneur relies on the ability of abstraction to identify opportunities for profit that are not apparent to the majority of the population (Kirzner, 1997). The entrepreneur 'upsets and disorganises' (Peter Drucker in Economist, 2009) and is a 'bold and imaginative deviator from established business patterns and practices' (ibid. and Baumol, 1968). The skills of abstraction which lead to disruptive entrepreneurial insights seem quite different to the administrative and cooperative skills required for management of an ongoing firm; but they also both stand apart from consideration of character traits that determine an individual's attitude to risk (see, for instance, Kihlstrom and Laffont, 1979). The self-employed will mix these ingredients in different proportions. At one end of the scale, an individual who is self-employed examining for a professional body may exhibit very little entrepreneurial activity. At the other end of the scale, a rapidly growing business that

2   Mises (1949) and Kirzner (1997) tend to distinguish (i) the entrepreneur from (ii and iii) capitalists and other businessmen, while Henry Schloss (1968) and others since (Casson, 2005) have suggested a distinction along these lines.

started a few years earlier with only one employee has probably benefited from a great deal of entrepreneurial insight.

The entrepreneurial insight – unknown unknowns

Equilibria could be defined as situations where we have an efficient allocation of resources, as defined by the state of preferences, costs of production and technology at a particular point in time. This information is widely known and transmitted to economic agents through various market signals (prices of goods, services, share prices, etc.). Let us consider the advent of information technology. In 1992 there were just under 11,000 self-employed computer analysts and programmers, and this had grown to just over 18,000 by 1998. In 2002 the figure had increased[3] to 51,000 (quarterly LFS, 1992, 1998 and 2002).

It would be hard to argue that all of these 51,000 self-employed individuals working in the UK were dotcom 'entrepreneurs'. Some may have been, but the majority will have spotted opportunities for profit in a range of market signals (such as wages) and supplied their labour accordingly. There was a long period of time when demand for IT consultants outstripped supply; a number of people spotted this disequilibrium (through the existence of inflated wages), became self-employed and moved the market to a new equilibrium. This describes a process of 'arbitrage', and in this sense the self-employed are helping the market to move towards equilibrium, but this does not describe 'entrepreneurial insight' of a radical kind.

---

3   And in the process the number of occupational categories expanded from computer analysts/consultants to occupations in 'information and communications technologies' and 'IT service delivery occupations'.

Consider those among these 51,000 who decided to become self-employed because they could see that the traditional role of many intermediaries (record companies, travel agents, insurance brokers, information providers, etc.) in the physical world was under threat, but that there would be a key role for intermediaries in the online world (see, for instance, Varian et al., 2007). This was an entrepreneurial insight that revealed an enormous potential from the reallocation of resources and, in each individual manifestation (Google, eBay, lastminute.com, Facebook, etc.), revealed a new allocation of resources which then led many self-employed IT consultants to work serving the enterprises started by these self-employed entrepreneurs. Only a small number out of the very large number of self-employed people are genuinely creating something new. For many self-employed, the process of contracting is not that different from the process of working for a firm.

This is the essential distinction between entrepreneurial insight and self-employment. What defines an entrepreneur is the ability to abstract and achieve insights that uncover apparent inefficient allocations of resources, when all other economic agents (including the self-employed) are observing an apparent equilibrium relationship (i.e. one defined by the present state of market information). Drawing on the ideas set out in Kirzner (1997) (and the words of Donald Rumsfeld), entrepreneurs are essential to the discovery of 'unknown unknowns' or the overcoming of 'sheer ignorance'. Many will fail, and it is not possible to know a priori which will succeed.

Thus, the self-employed are not all predominantly entrepreneurs, even if they are considering price signals and working to arbitrage alternative opportunities. They are, however, part of the mechanisms that move markets towards new equilibria working within the signals of the market. Essentially, most of the self-employed, like most employees, discover the 'known unknowns'.

The entrepreneur changes the very nature of information, knowledge and understanding by working outside of the signals provided by the price mechanism. The entrepreneur, at the point of discovery, cannot, by definition, be following the price signals of the market as the entrepreneurial insights they arrive at uncover these signals as being incorrect. Such entrepreneurial insight is spread very thinly among the self-employed.

Having distinguished that not all the self-employed are providing entrepreneurial skills, the real question is how important is self-employment as a route through which entrepreneurial skill is supplied to the economy? At first this may seem a bit of an unusual question, as the idea that the innovative or entrepreneurial input is provided by smaller firms and start-ups is pervasive (see, for instance, OECD, 2004). The creative destruction of Schumpeter, where new entrepreneurial firms spring up to 'disturb the economic status quo through innovations' (Chell et al., 1991: 22),[4] is often taken as a given.

This view of ageing, large firms not being engaged in the process of entrepreneurship is not, however, universal. The original challenge in many ways came from Schumpeter himself, as his approach to entrepreneurship changed from one that emphasised small firms and individuals in the process of entrepreneurship to one that 'include[d] large established corporations and government agencies as agglomerations capable of fulfilling the entrepreneurial function' (Frank, 1998). In an extension of

---

4   As cited in Goss (2005).

this, Acs and Audretsch (2005) draw on a quote from Galbraith (1956: 86): 'There is no more pleasant fiction than that technological change is the product of the matchless ingenuity of the small man forced by competition to employ his wits to better his neighbour.'

Our previous discussion suggests a clear differentiation between concepts of technological change and the entrepreneurial function,[5] but the essential challenge has remained and is alive today. Commentators such as Howard Stevenson have suggested that corporations can have entrepreneurship at their centre, through the development of entrepreneurial managers (Stevenson and Jarillo, 1990). Some of this debate is, at least partly, driven by a definition of entrepreneurship that incorporates a wider range of activities, as Stevenson suggests that entrepreneurship is 'the pursuit of opportunity beyond the resources you currently control' (Economist, 2009).

If, however, we are to consider the extent to which the entrepreneurial input is likely to be supplied by new start-ups (and therefore the self-employed) as opposed to existing firms which attempt to foster (what is often called) 'intrapreneurship', we need first to consider the theory of firm formation. Only then can we debate whether the environment of an ongoing firm represents a fertile ground for the development and nurturing of entrepreneurship.

---

5   Technological innovation in itself is often a destroyer of jobs as it immediately renders obsolete a host of working practices and sometimes entire sectors. The entrepreneur, however (who is not necessarily innovator or inventor), is then essential in the process of spotting these newly defined disequilibria (inefficient allocations of resources) and moving us towards new, more efficient uses of land, labour and capital. Innovation and entrepreneurship are separate concepts, but often not easily distinguished.

Entrepreneurship and the firm

In his 1937 paper for *Economica*, Coase begins by describing an economic system that 'works itself', or, as he put it in his 1991 Nobel laureate lecture, the 'decentralised system of organisation focused on prices'. Coase was not, however, happy with the lack of detail on why and how firms operate within this neoclassical paradigm.[6] While on a fellowship to the USA during 1931/32 his observations led him to describe the process of firm formation that eventually became known as transaction cost economics (see Williamson, 2005, for a detailed review and history of this work).

Coase (1937) asked why we observe firms. As suggested in the previous section of this study, the price mechanism provides the signals that are needed for independent economic agents to organise production, distribution and consumption. In this world where the market carries out the organisation function, the firm is something of an anomaly, as it is an alternative (bureaucratic) form of organisation. Put another way, inside the firm there are many different processes being directed by the business manager/owner and they must be organising the factors of production to achieve a set of outcomes more efficiently (i.e. at a lower cost) than if they are left to the price mechanism and independent agents. The insight that Coase brought in 1937 was that this situation can arise because there 'is a cost of using the price mechanism'.

The ideas of Ronald Coase have been taken forward and developed by a variety of commentators, including Oliver Williamson, who also received a Nobel Prize for his work in 2009. Transaction cost economics explains why the firm exists, through identification of the costs associated with coordination of independent

6   Coase draws on the comments of Lionel Robbins and others to suggest that he was not the first to feel uneasy about this lack of detail.

agents within the market system – for instance, the issues of contractual enforcement (between various actors working under contract for services) and the costs involved in securing the 'right' prices for goods and services. In this instance, at any one point in time, the firm exists because (i) it carries out the functions of providing a good or service at a cost that is lower than would be observed if left to the market (i.e. taking into account the costs of transaction) and (ii) no other firm is carrying out these functions at a lower cost (Williamson, 2005). To survive, the firm must represent a more efficient alternative than other firms or the price mechanism.

Within this framework, let us go back to our theory of entrepreneurial discovery in an inherently unknowing world. The very nature of that moment of entrepreneurial insight (when apparent equilibria are revealed as disequilibria) is one gained independently of any price signals – for the truly entrepreneurial, the price mechanism is no guide. If we assume that the entrepreneur (or a sponsor) took on the risk of funding the opportunity for profit that flows from the entrepreneurial insight, why would they choose to start a firm, as opposed to using the market mechanism?

At first sight, the concept of transaction costs as a justification for the setting up of a firm may seem irrelevant in this setting. We have an entrepreneur with a genuinely new insight, which neither the market of itself, nor any other firm, is providing. The process of organising factors of production so as to best take advantage of the original entrepreneurial insight is, in itself, however, a process of discovery. There is a period of experimentation with different forms of organisation/production and at this point, transaction costs will be high. There will be no shared understanding (or information) between the participants in production/organisation of what is required of each of them. At the initial point of development, the protagonists all have independent knowledge that needs to be collated and coordinated. The costs of going back and forth to the various individuals who are making components/organising service delivery are likely to render subcontracting arrangements prohibitively expensive. In addition, while patents and intellectual property rights afford some protection, they are in effect an additional transaction cost.

In the early stages of development, when bringing an entrepreneurial insight to market, consideration of the high transaction costs that result from a lack of shared knowledge and understanding renders the firm the only effective choice of organisation. As this process of experimentation leads to standardisation of processes within the firm, however, there is a continual lowering of these transaction costs. Many of the components are likely to soon become standardised commodities outside the company (see Williamson, 2002, for more detail on the sort of transaction firms are likely to internalise).

As the new information and understanding represented by the original entrepreneurial insight becomes common knowledge, transaction costs continue to fall to a level that may eventually threaten the firm's very survival. This is akin to the idea of the transient entrepreneurial rents ascribed by many contributors to the subject of entrepreneurship (see, for instance, Carter, 2009). The firm's continuing survival would then seem to depend very much on operational issues (including, for instance, the protection and development of brands – Urwin et al., 2008b) and the key skills and abilities it relies on at this point are those of the business administrator and manager.

Does the firm recruit entrepreneurs?
1. The proposition is that adaptation is the central problem of economic organization;
2. That adaptations within firms are of a cooperative kind and are accomplished in a 'conscious, deliberate, purposeful' way through administration;
3. A theory of authority, with emphasis on mutual gain and consent of the governed;
4. Requisite flexibility is accomplished by negotiating a cost-effective 'zone of acceptance', within which employees are presumed to adapt cooperatively;
5. Informal organization arose spontaneously in conjunction with and as a support for formal organization and furthermore afforded protection for personal integrity. An economy of pecuniary and nonpecuniary incentives was a unifying concept throughout.

Source: Williamson (1990) drawing on Barnard (1938)

Old firms, new firms and skill of entrepreneurship

The suggestion is that older firms will be demanding a certain mix of skills that seem a long way from those associated with entrepreneurship. Consider, for instance, some of the insights suggested by Chester Barnard (1938), as set out in Williamson (1990) (see above).

When considering the processes of administration within the firm suggested by Barnard, there is an emphasis on cooperation, acceptance and the adherence to a system. The implication is that the firm requires those who have an acceptance of authority and are willing to work within clear parameters: this seems to be almost diametrically opposed to the definition of an entrepreneur. Firms are set up around the initial entrepreneurial insight and, as this idea ages, it is business managers that are required to administer employees, who cooperate and negotiate to ensure that the firm carries out functions more efficiently than the market. Some employees will be tasked with providing the strategic insights that influence the nature of the company and keep it running, but they are not there to unearth the unknown unknowns.

One of the few opportunities for individuals to supply the skills of entrepreneurship to the economy would seem to be through self-employment, as the entrepreneurship required of employees in older (usually large) firms would seem limited. The entrepreneurial input is the central concept around which the firm is initially constituted. Similarly, in the first stages of firm formation (i.e. in younger firms) there would seem to be more room for entrepreneurial input from employees as the specifics of organisation, production or distribution have yet to be decided. As the firm ages, its continued survival is based on management of transaction costs, brand and other functions of business administration. This is not to suggest that there is no room for innovation, insight and originality in these functions, but there would seem to be little room for entrepreneurship in the pure sense.[7]

We have a clear firm life cycle. At first, organisation of production around the original entrepreneurial insight is the primary reason for choosing to set up a firm, but not its main source of

---

7   Large firms in their 'employee engagement' plans may try to capture entrepreneurial ability, but firms use educational qualifications to place individuals within the bureaucracy – any entrepreneurial ability among their workforce would be purely serendipitous. As with the approach of Baumol (1968), we suggest that there is a distinction between the managerial and entrepreneurial functions.

A case of entrepreneurship

Steven Paul 'Steve' Jobs was born 24 February 1955, is the co-founder and former CEO of Apple Incorporated and previously served as CEO of Pixar Animation Studios. He has worked for large companies and is, arguably, highly entrepreneurial. But his career trajectory involved leaving and then being brought back to Apple, which redeveloped its business model.

In the late 1970s, Jobs, with Apple co-founder Steve Wozniak, created one of the first commercially successful personal computers. In the early 1980s, Jobs was among the first to see the commercial potential of the mouse-driven graphical user interface. After losing a power struggle with the board of directors in 1985, however, Jobs resigned from Apple and founded NeXT, which was subsequently bought in 1997 by Apple Computer Inc., at which point Jobs took up the role as Apple CEO again. Steve Jobs was listed as *Fortune* magazine's Most Powerful Businessman of 2007 and at that point Apple had approximately 20,000 employees.

In 1986, Jobs purchased the division of Lucasfilm Ltd which focused on computer graphics, and spun it off as Pixar Animation Studios. He remained CEO and majority shareholder until its acquisition by the Walt Disney Company in 2006. Disney paid $7.4 billion for Pixar.

rent. As the firm ages the economic rent that is gained from the originality of the entrepreneurial insight dissipates; from this point, justification of the firm's existence becomes based on efficient organisation, and the skills of the workforce reflect this. If we introduce a disruptive technology or idea into this framework, the older firm's focus on administration and functionality, not entrepreneurial skills, does not leave it well placed. In considering this process of growth from start-up to ageing firm, and the way it is likely to have an impact on the skills that are demanded, we arrive at a Schumpeterian world. Creative destruction is driven by the arrival of new firms and their entrepreneurial insights; in contrast to older firms whose skills base is such that they are unlikely to be able to reinvent themselves.

During the last decade many famous CEOs have been found somewhat wanting when firms require a rethink of their entire business model. This is another manifestation of the differences between small and large firms in that, among the latter, managers and CEOs are promoted primarily on their organisational skills and ability to facilitate this internal cooperative machine. When the environment changes to such an extent that they have to draw on entrepreneurial insights, they are often found lacking. When firms require change they often bring back their original entrepreneurial founders.

Conclusion

There are a number of key insights that flow from this discussion:

- Entrepreneurial skills will not be especially sought after by large firms. In a modern economy where education has evolved primarily to serve firms and government, entrepreneurship is unlikely to be valued or promoted in the same way as other skills (whether specific or transferable) that arise from the education system.[8] In fact, the skill of

---

8   Even if we thought that entrepreneurial skills were being demanded by older firms, there is a question over how individuals would signal entrepreneurial

entrepreneurial insight, by its very nature, is unlikely to be demanded and supplied within the economy in predictable ways, as that skill works outside the signals provided by the price mechanism.

- For individuals whose entrepreneurial ability is accompanied by other skills and abilities, the education system may still be an attractive proposition to develop their skills. These other skills and abilities will help the individual progress through the educational system and secure some return on this investment. For those whose abilities are primarily related to entrepreneurial insight, however, the educational qualifications system may not be an attractive proposition or a valid way of signalling skills.

- This leaves self-employment as one of the few routes for the supply of entrepreneurial skills to the economy. We cannot rule out the possibility that individuals who possess (i) the skills of abstraction and identification of entrepreneurial opportunities are also those who are (ii) risk-loving and/or (iii) good managers and administrators. It is also possible that entrepreneurial insight is closely correlated with other skills and forms of educational ability. Even given this, however, there would seem to be some real potential for loss of entrepreneurial ability to the economy if self-employment and the development of small firms with employees are discouraged.

- The possibility of securing venture capital is an option

---

ability. When we think of what might constitute a credible signal of entrepreneurial ability, gaining a qualification in business and management would not seem to be one of them. In contrast, having a period of successful self-employment or working in a new start-up firm seem to be some of the few ways that such signals of entrepreneurial ability could be provided.

open to relatively few start-ups. Furthermore, having entrepreneurial insight, but not the skills to run a business, may result in failure (even when the entrepreneurial insight is valid). Given this, there would seem to be a relatively high probability that even viable entrepreneurial insights will fail to prosper. Here we can see a role for the serial entrepreneur who may fail repeatedly.

- For those who possess the skill of entrepreneurship, but are more risk averse, taking up an employee job in a large firm (and gaining a reward for other skills) represents a loss of entrepreneurial skill to the economy.

This is a relatively simplistic view of the world and the reality is much less clear cut. For instance, the skill of 'entrepreneurial insight' is likely to be one that can be put to other uses. This mirrors the approach of Baumol (1990), whose historical study suggests that the entrepreneurs are always with us, but that when they face economic systems that do not present an outlet or return to their entrepreneurial skills they turn to much less productive activities. The entrepreneurial are always with us; we cannot increase their numbers in the population, but we can ensure that the economic systems and institutions we have in place provide them with the incentive to engage in entrepreneurship.

Those with special entrepreneurial insights are incredibly dispersed, even among the population of self-employed. It would seem in some ways that our truly successful entrepreneur is something of a 'black swan' (Taleb, 2007), as he meets two of the criteria, of being apparently unpredictable and having a substantial impact. Predicting from where entrepreneurs will come is impractical. After the fact we may expect to observe certain skills and abilities among the successful, but among those who started out on this road (with these skills and abilities) we would be hard pressed to pick winners. This leads to support of unfettered experimentation (or creative destruction) as possibly the only viable approach to gaining the fruits of entrepreneurship. In the spirit of Hayek (Hayek's 1974 Nobel lecture),[9] the suggestion is that the limited insight we can get from this acceptance is preferable to the existing misplaced certainty we have over job creation and destruction.

---

9   Hayek suggested that 'I prefer true but imperfect knowledge, even if it leaves much undetermined and unpredictable, to a pretence of exact knowledge that is likely to be false'.

6 CONCLUSIONS AND IMPLICATIONS FOR POLICY

Self-employment versus employment

In many senses, self-employment is simply an alternative to working as an employee which may be economically more desirable in particular circumstances. From the point of view of both the employer and the individual, self-employment (or a contract for services) is a relatively simple and unfettered form of working when compared with the modern-day employer–employee relationship (or contract of service). An employment relationship involves a wider subordination of the employee in exchange for the provision of greater security and other benefits.

For the self-employed individual, the benefits associated with working for oneself, which derive from the control over working arrangements, also entail greater responsibility and an increase in risk. This trade-off has been at the heart of debates over whether the self-employed are pulled into self-employment because of, for instance, the attraction of being their own boss or are pushed to consider this form of working as a result of the barriers they face when attempting to secure an employee job.

Barriers to the securing of an employee job can include discrimination, a lack of formal qualifications (even when individuals possess the required skills and abilities they may be unable to signal this to potential employers) or the potentially scarring effects of unemployment and inactivity. Thus, many specific groups of individuals have a higher level of representation among the self-employed than in the population as a whole. Self-employment accounts, for example, for 42 per cent of males who are active in the labour market and aged 65 or above. It is also particularly prevalent among first-generation immigrants and those for whom English is not their first language.

Self-employment can be regarded as a 'safety valve' for those who cannot supply their skills to the market because of barriers they face in becoming an employee. As such, self-employment should not be made difficult as a result of tax rules and other artificial impediments.

In fact, the barriers to self-employment without employees in the UK are comparatively few, though some have argued that pursuit of the 'false' self-employed by HM Revenue and Customs may act as a disincentive. The self-employed do benefit from certain tax advantages and, in instances where HMRC feel that there is a case to be answered, the focus of prosecution is on the self-employed individual rather than on the firm that is purchasing the services. Given that the self-employed forgo holiday pay, sick leave and a variety of other benefits in return for a slightly more generous tax treatment, the focus of prosecution would seem somewhat unfair. It is also the case that the self-employed have the opportunity to characterise labour income as income from capital (which can be taxed at a lower rate). These issues are best addressed by fundamental reform, and the recent Mirrlees Review of taxation sets out some of the key challenges. The prospect of National Insurance contributions being removed as a separate category of tax or National Insurance benefits being tied more closely to contributions would better ensure that there is no net advantage or disadvantage from being self-employed.

Recent reviews of the administration and effectiveness of HM Revenue and Customs have been particularly scathing.[1] The department has undergone continual change since its formation in April 2005; it has the worst staff engagement performance of the entire Civil Service;[2] and there are concerns over the effectiveness of management. In contrast to the calls we make elsewhere in this text for government departments to cut their activities, we would argue that HMRC is under-resourced and cannot cope with the administration of an increasingly unwieldy tax regime.

In the present environment we have an increasingly complicated tax code and 'deficiencies in the underlying legislation'[3] which lead to increased uncertainty for taxpayers and HMRC. This often distracts HMRC from its core mission to collect tax that is due under the law and leads to expensive court cases (see, for instance, HMRC's long-running battle with Arctic Systems). An effective and efficient tax collection agency is essential to the workings of a modern economy. At present the uncertain environment in which HMRC operates acts as a brake on entrepreneurship. The cuts in funding serve to transfer more of the costs of compliance to firms and individuals, while the work of those in HMRC who are tasked with identifying evasion and avoidance remains underfunded. The result is that honest taxpayers pay more.

---

1   See, for instance, HM Treasury, *The Administration and Effectiveness of HM Revenue and Customs*, Treasury 16th Report, 2011.

2   Civil Service People Survey, 2010.

3   Ibid.

The regulation of firms

The potential combined effects of the tax system and regulation are to push the distribution of firms towards the extremes of self-employed with no employees and to raise the minimum average size of firms among those with employees. Individuals may be further 'pushed' into self-employment as the regulatory impositions on companies that employ individuals reduce the job opportunities that they are able to create. This will increase the number of self-employed and potentially make the position of such self-employed persons even less secure than if they had been employed under a legal framework in which there was much less employment regulation within firms.

According to a British Chambers of Commerce survey in June 2011, one in three small-business owners who are looking to expand are put off by the costs of employment law, complying with the new National Employment Savings Trust scheme and so on. The same proportion suggested that they would expand if given exemptions from these rules. To some extent, of course, the same constraints might apply to larger firms. Regulation acts as a fixed cost, however, and artificially penalises small firms relative to large firms. This is a distortion of the market and, potentially, an impediment to competition. The burden that regulation places on small firms means that, as already noted, there may be people who become self-employed when they would prefer to be employed. It also means that there are people who are self-employed without employees when, in a less regulated market, they would prefer to be self-employed with employees. This is detrimental to such self-employed people, but it also closes off opportunities to those groups that may find employment with small firms easier to access than employment within large firms. Small firms tend to employ more part-time workers, more women, more of the oldest and youngest, more people who regard English as a barrier to employment and more poorly educated people. Inhibiting the growth of small firms can therefore cut off an important route to prosperity for those who do not have the qualifications and background to succeed in other parts of the labour market.

Insofar as regulation is an impediment to the growth of small firms it is also an impediment to entrepreneurship and the process of new job creation in the economy as a whole. At any one point in time new firms or start-ups account for a large proportion of net job creation. While this net gain is at the expense of a lot of job destruction, the young firms that rise from this firmament grow more rapidly and create more jobs than older firms. Predicting in advance which firms will create jobs is impossible, however. In the UK, it is likely that just 6 per cent of firms create over half of all new jobs, and there is less than a one-in-a-thousand chance that a new firm will become a large firm. Special initiatives to encourage particular types of small firms are not likely to be successful. On the other hand, a generalised reduction in regulation that inhibits the growth of small firms is important. This is one of our most important policy conclusions. Regulation prevents the development of large enterprises from small enterprises, but it acts in a way that we cannot observe because the enterprises that never develop are invisible.

The costs of regulation

It is very difficult to calculate the costs of regulation, for many reasons. For example, insofar as people are able to change their business models to reduce the impact of regulation, costs can be reduced. On the other hand, some of the costs of regulation are hidden as their impact on the economy is on the entrepreneurial opportunities that are not exploited because of the burden of regulation – these missed entrepreneurial opportunities can never be known. Various studies have attempted to calculate the costs of regulation and, however imperfect, the results are instructive. For instance, the total administrative cost of regulation to businesses has been estimated at nearly £112 billion or 7.9 per cent of GDP in 2011 (Institute of Directors, 2011), and the total net cost to business of the major UK and EU regulations that have been approved since 1998 is £88.3 billion. Despite indications to the contrary from government, the burden continues to grow. According to the British Chambers of Commerce, using the government's own figures, employment regulations brought in by the UK government will cost firms a total of £22.87 billion between now and 2015.

As suggested in this study, many of the existing micro-evaluations which attempt to gauge the impact of regulation on small businesses adopt flawed methods. The same arguments often apply as those suggested in the area of tax compliance, however, in that regulation acts as a fixed cost with a disproportionate burden on small business. Chittenden et al. (2002) show that the burden of tax compliance as a proportion of turnover bears sixteen times more heavily on the smallest businesses than on the largest.

The 2011 budget was styled as a budget for growth and deregulation. The measures proposed are unlikely to have had a significant impact, however. For instance, it was announced that 100 pages would be cut from the tax code, but this is less than 1 per cent of a tax code that by some measures is the longest in the world. Furthermore, regulations that were cut tended to be those with a more limited scope: one of the tax regulations that was cut affected only one firm. Employment regulations costing businesses £350 million were abolished but, again, we can see that this is a drop in the ocean compared with the existing regulation and the increase in regulation that we are expecting over the coming few years. Finally, there was a moratorium announced on new business regulation for businesses with fewer than ten employees for three years. Again, this makes no dent in the existing accumulated regulatory burden.

Reducing regulation

Given that regulation appears to be a fixed cost and therefore, arguably, discriminates against small firms, it is often suggested that there should be differential regulatory treatment of firms according to either age and/or size. Employers have traditionally had a range of more flexible employment models available, such as employing individuals on short-term temporary contracts. Employment protection legislation has increasingly closed these routes, however. This has reduced the flexibility available to employers. It is not just the cost of regulation but the risks of regulation which bear heavily on small firms. Small firms have less flexibility to redeploy staff should one part of the business suffer from reduced turnover or if employees have extended periods of absence that are mandated by regulation. At the same time, employees in smaller firms have a much more equal relationship with their employer, as they are a significant factor in the operations of the firm, contributing a substantial proportion of the labour input. Evidence also suggests that the employees of small businesses, which have less formalised processes, are actually happier. Again, this would point to the possibility that, even if employment regulation were justified in general – something that many IEA authors would regard as contestable – different approaches are needed for small and large firms.

Given the state of the economy and the need to spur growth through entrepreneurship, we must grasp the nettle and start to consider specific areas where smaller firms and 'start-ups' may be able to gain specific exemptions. For instance:

- The penalties for employing illegal immigrants throw an enforcement burden on to business that may be disproportionately harsh for small firms.
- The right to request flexible working; the right to request time off for training; statutory holidays and the minimum wage for those aged under 21 – all impact much more heavily on small firms, which have less leeway for staff redeployment. The existence of these rights raises the risks of employment for small firms.
- Conditions surrounding internships could be relaxed for small firms. For example, they could be allowed to pay some form of retainer below the minimum wage for a period of time. This could allow students and those re-entering the labour market to gain work experience and therefore reduce the risks of taking on employees who do not have a recent work history.
- Small firms could be exempt from requirements under the National Employment Savings Trust pension arrangements that require auto-enrolment, compulsory deductions from employees' pay packets and will, when fully rolled out, require employer contributions.

- Product market regulation is also onerous for small businesses and exemptions should be considered. This is an area where wholesale reform is required as the present system has an inbuilt incentive for the creation of regulation (as the onus is to 'protect' the consumer/employee), with little incentive to consider the costs to business.
- With regard to the tax system, simplification is the key. The removal of a number of tax reliefs would reduce compliance costs for small businesses. In considering the alignment of the corporation tax rate with the income tax rate (and hence the removal of special treatment for small companies), however, one must be careful that those small firms engaged in employment generation are not negatively impacted.
- Small firms should be able to discuss retirement arrangements with employees without the threat of age-discrimination legislation being invoked.
- Small firms should be permitted to write temporary contracts of employment and employ agency workers without employment rights accruing.

In the areas listed some readers may feel that there are fundamental rights being potentially undermined. Suggested exemptions for small firms from some of the provisions on maternity leave or the National Employment Savings Trust pension scheme may seem to affect vulnerable groups. Such regulation and legislation, however, as well as increasing the costs of creating jobs generally, makes specific groups more costly to employ. Governments legislate for more rights for certain groups of employees, but they fail to compensate employers fully for the increased costs that this implies. This directly undermines the very aim of the legislation. Furthermore, a disproportionate amount of this extra burden is borne by small firms which are more likely to be creating job opportunities for disadvantaged groups. Legislating that small firms follow all of these rules that are designed to protect the disadvantaged means many of the jobs they would create are simply not created.

Some of these proposals would need an amendment to EU regulation. Many of them, however, could be implemented by the UK government. Exemptions for small firms are an imperfect step, and it may be desirable to extend exemptions to larger firms too. Indeed, it could be argued that exemptions for small firms would artificially distort the market in favour of small firms. Small-business exemptions have four advantages, however. First, regulations act as a 'poll tax' on businesses that discriminates against smaller companies. Secondly, such exemptions allow us to experiment in a controlled way with less regulation and may give politicians confidence that they can reduce regulation more generally while taking fewer risks. Thirdly, such exemptions from regulation would lead to a situation that better reflects the realities of employee relations in small firms, where each individual employee is much more important to the survival of the firm, and therefore managers are more focused on ensuring good relations. In a small firm job security requires the survival of the firm and cannot, generally, be legislated for. This whole approach reduces the likelihood that we will strangle the big firms of the future at birth and is likely to create greater competition in the labour market, which, in turn, undermines many of the key arguments in favour of regulation.

One simple way of dealing with these regulatory exemptions would be to provide a standardised part of an employment contract that listed the regulations from which a small business was exempt and directed employees to a government website for further information regarding the detail. However, in pursuing this issue of exemptions from various forms of employment protection legislation, we are essentially moving towards a recommendation that small companies be able to employ staff as self-employed individuals. The staff involved would register under one of the forms of self-employment status discussed previously, and this would reduce the burden of regulation and legislation associated with small firms' generation of employment. As is reflected in the discussion of this issue by various commentators (see for example the discussion instigated by Pirie on the Adam Smith Institute blog[4]), one needs to consider a number of issues of detail, but practice in the US and within the construction industry provides examples of how this might be taken forward.

The government could supplement this approach with the subsidisation of specialist services that deal with taxation, human resources regulation and product-market regulation. In many ways this is part of the role that bodies such as the Federation of Small Businesses take on, but firms pay for this out of their own pockets. There is a case that at least some of the cost should be borne by the government departments that impose the regulatory burdens. This has the added advantage of making more of the costs of regulation explicit to taxpayers.

It is highly likely that many of the employees who are taken on if regulations are relaxed would otherwise have been temporary workers, contractors or self-employed. It is by no means certain that the situation of those who have contract-for-service, or

4   http://www.adamsmith.org/blog/tax-and-economy/a-small-step-to-a-big-improvement/

contract-of-service, relationships with small businesses will be facing greater overall risks as a result of these proposals.

Entrepreneurship and small firms

No policy measures can help us predict and support entrepreneurs who will be successful. This is not something that will be rectified as econometrics improves; rather, it is a result of the nature of the entrepreneurial process. Policy needs to ensure that entrepreneurial experiments are not discouraged in general – there is no sense in which winners can be picked in advance by encouraging particular firms or types of firms.

Serial entrepreneurship is also important. Entrepreneurs learn 'on the job'. Some failed ventures serve as learning experiences for those who subsequently move on to be successful. It should be noted also that the self-employed are not all entrepreneurs in the genuine sense. Policies that promote entrepreneurship and policies that promote self-employment are not necessarily the same. Policies that promote education and training may also not necessarily promote entrepreneurship. The best policy regime for encouraging entrepreneurship is one that has the fewest regulatory barriers to business entry and development. We have to accept that the process of job creation and entrepreneurship involves failure which may seem wasteful. Such failure, however, is a necessary part of the process of discovering the successes. The nature of entrepreneurial insight is such that it is unique, original and often seemingly outlandish (for example, the invention of Post-it notes). We can create environments to allow entrepreneurship to flourish, but we do not possess the knowledge and understanding to effectively manage the process.

The nature of the self-employment/employee choice is such that even those who possess a more risk-loving disposition may be put off starting their own business, because of the lack of information on the parameters of the self-employment 'gamble'. Those with entrepreneurial insight are unlikely to put this skill to work as an employee in older firms. The structure of older (predominantly large) firms is such that they do not generally provide opportunities for advancement of more entrepreneurial employees.

Entrepreneurial insight that is successfully applied alerts economic actors to a new, more efficient allocation of resources that can be said to benefit many more people than the individuals themselves. While successful entrepreneurs may become wealthy, the value of their insight provides positive external benefits (or spillovers) for the whole of society. From an economist's perspective, we may consider that the marginal social benefits of entrepreneurship often outweigh the marginal private benefits.

Policy implications

For many individuals, self-employment and the creation of a new business (becoming self-employed with employees) are the only ways to operationalise their entrepreneurial insight. Very few have access to the sort of administrative and financial support that comes with backing from venture capitalists. It is important that the recommendations suggested above are adopted because regulation is effectively a tax on the application of entrepreneurial insight. If entrepreneurial insight has spillover benefits, it is especially important that the development of such insights is not taxed – both explicitly and through the regulatory burden that is applied to entrepreneurs.

Given the nature of entrepreneurship, the government should

cease to spend money on programmes that actively promote entre-preneurship among schoolchildren and adults and on research that is intended to calculate the amount of entrepreneurship in the economy and how this is changing. Government is not well positioned to effect a change in the way that popular culture views entrepreneurship and self-employment, and therefore promotional activities are not likely to be an effective use of public funds – espe-cially as those programmes will probably be delivered in state insti-tutions that are far from the coalface of entrepreneurship. Insofar as the government funds further and adult education at all, there is no reason why part of such programmes should not involve training in basic business practices of accounting, cash-flow management, writing business plans and so on, as entrepreneurial insight may be lost to the economy because of poor business management. This does not require any change from current policy.

There is a case for the government levelling the playing field between the support it gives to entrepreneurs and the support it gives to formal qualifications. For example, a scheme could be created alongside the one that presently supports students to go to university that enables people who have reached a given level of qualification at age eighteen to access public funds to start up a business. The same rules would apply as apply to a student loan, with repayment conditional on the borrower achieving an acceptable (£21,000) level of annual income. Only one such loan could be accessed in a person's lifetime. This scheme would help to overcome liquidity constraints which are probably even greater in the market for funds for entrepreneurship than in the market for funds for higher education. The provision of loans would probably lead to fewer deadweight and other losses as the loan would be paid back by those who succeed (as opposed to the

present situation, where special tax breaks or subsidies can be taken up by those who are not entrepreneurial or who are simply attempting to avoid higher taxation). An income-contingent loan is preferable, in the author's view, to greater leniency in bankruptcy laws which have the perverse effect of reducing the incentives for lenders to invest in start-ups. It should also be noted that any externalities arising from entrepreneurship are likely to be greater than those arising from higher education, and such a programme would incentivise and orient those of school-leaving age towards entrepreneurship, much more than existing promotional programmes. In the long term the scheme could be made fiscally neutral given that there would be a wide pool of diversified risks being supported in this way.

While such a scheme may have much to recommend it – especially given that the middle of the qualifications distribution seems the most likely to take up self-employment – it still suggests a 'gauntlet' approach. That is, those who do not have the ability or disposition to achieve in education but still have entrepreneurial insight, as well as the existing self-employed who face barriers to employing workers, would not be eligible. In these instances one may consider the addition of a programme akin to the Enterprise Allowance Scheme (EAS) of the 1980s, but with larger sums on offer and repayment expected on the achievement of a certain level of income. This would overcome the potential for liquidity constraints of many who find themselves stuck in self-employment without employees.

Conclusion

One interventionist measure has been proposed here which levels the playing field that is currently tilted against entrepreneurship and in favour of formal education. This measure – the provision of government loan guarantees – also deals with the liquidity constraints and uncertainty associated with the uncovering of 'unknown unknowns', which is central to the process of entrepreneurship. Whether this proposal for a government-guaranteed loan system would be possible in the present fiscal environment is questionable. What it does emphasise is the need to orient individuals towards the idea of entrepreneurship with real incentives. It is perhaps the other policy proposals of this monograph, however, which provide the most effective tools for the promotion of entrepreneurship, as the stripping away of regulation that small businesses face does not represent a cost to the exchequer. Some will argue that there is a potential cost to those groups whose rights are protected by such regulation and legislation; but in small firms the protection of employees is guaranteed only by the survival of the firm.

The government cannot select winners or even develop schemes that will successfully nurture entrepreneurial skills. The government can, however, remove barriers to entrepreneurship. Regulation is a particularly important barrier because it bears most heavily on new, growing, small and entrepreneurial firms. Such policies of deregulation are important for other reasons too. They will particularly assist people who are otherwise at a disadvantage in heavily regulated labour markets and they will ensure that formal employment in small businesses is not artificially discouraged. More generally, a policy of stripping away regulations that affect small businesses will ensure that entrepreneurship – the engine of growth and the hub of a free economy – can thrive.

REFERENCES

Acs, Z. J. and D. B. Audretsch (2005), 'Entrepreneurship and innovation', Summer Institute of the Entrepreneurship, Growth and Public Policy Division of the Max Planck Institute of Economics.

Ahmad, N. (2006), *A proposed framework for business demographic statistics*, Paris: OECD Statistics Working Paper Series.

Aker, A. (2004), 'Discriminant analysis of default risk', MPRA Paper no. 1002.

Alpin, C. and P. Urwin (1996), 'Atypical employment in the capital', *Labour Market Briefing*, University of Westminster/London Chamber of Commerce and Industry, December.

Altman, E. (1968), 'Financial ratios, discriminant analysis and the prediction of corporate bankruptcy', *Journal of Finance*, September, pp. 589–609.

Anyadike-Danes, M., K. Bonner, M. Hart and C. Mason (2009), 'Measuring business growth: high-growth firms and their contribution to employment in the UK', Research report, National Endowment for Science, Technology and the Arts, October.

Audretsch, D. (2007), 'Entrepreneurship capital and economic growth', *Oxford Review of Economic Policy*, 23(1): 63–78.

Audretsch, D. B., L. Klomp, E. Santarelli and A. R. Thurik (2004), 'Gibrat's Law: are the services different?', *Review of Industrial Organization*, 24: 301–24.

Barnard, C. (1938), *The Functions of the Executive*, Cambridge, MA: Harvard University Press (fifteenth printing, 1962).

Barnes, M. and J. Haskel (2002a), 'The sources of productivity growth: micro-level evidence for the OECD', National Statistics Productivity Workshop.

Barnes, M. and J. Haskel (2002b), 'Job creation, job destruction and the contribution of small businesses: evidence for UK manufacturing', Working Paper no. 461, Queen Mary Department of Economics.

Bates, T. (1990), 'Entrepreneur human capital inputs and small business longevity', *Review of Economics and Statistics*, 72(4): 551–9.

Baumol, W. J. (1968), 'Entrepreneurship in economic theory', *American Economic Review*, 58(2), Papers and Proceedings of the Eightieth Annual Meeting of the American Economic Association (May), pp. 64–71.

Baumol, W. J. (1990), 'Entrepreneurship: productive, unproductive, and destructive', *Journal of Political Economy*, 98(5): 893–921.

Bertrand, M. and S. Mullainathan (2004), 'Are Emily and Greg more employable than Lakisha and Jamal? A field experiment on labor market discrimination', *American Economic Review*, 94(4): 991.

Birch, D. L. (1979), *The Job Generation Process*, Unpublished report prepared by the MIT Program on Neighborhood and Regional Change for the Economic Development

Administration, US Department of Commerce, Washington, DC.

Birch, D. L. (1981), 'Who creates jobs?', *The Public Interest*, 65: 3–14.

Birch, D. L. (1987), *Job Creation in America: How Our Smallest Companies Put the Most People to Work*, New York: Free Press.

Blackaby, D., D. Leslie, P. Murphy and N. O'Leary (1998), 'The ethnic wage gap and employment differentials in the 1990s: evidence for Britain', *Economics Letters*, 58: 97–103.

Blackburn, R. and A. Kovalainen (2009), 'Researching small firms and entrepreneurship: past, present and future', *International Journal of Management Reviews*, 11(2): 127–48.

Blackburn, R. and D. Smallbone (2008), 'Researching small firms and entrepreneurship in the UK: developments and distinctiveness', *Entrepreneurship Theory and Practice*, 32(2): 267–88.

Blanchflower, D. (2000), 'Self-employment in OECD countries', *Labour Economics*, 7: 471–505.

Blanchflower, D. (2004), 'Self-employment: more may not be better', Paper presented at the Conference on Self-employment organised by the Economic Council of Sweden, March.

Blanchflower, D. (2007), 'Recent developments in the UK economy: the economics of walking about', Bernard Corry Memorial Lecture, Queen Mary, University of London, 30 May.

Blanchflower, D. and A. Oswald (1998), 'What makes an entrepreneur?', *Journal of Labor Economics*, 16(1): 26–60.

Blanchflower, D. G., P. Levine and D. Zimmerman (2003), 'Discrimination in the small business credit market', *Review of Economics and Statistics*, 85(4): 930–43.

Blanchflower, D. G., A. J. Oswald and A. Stutzer (2001), 'Latent entrepreneurship across nations', *European Economic Review*, 45(4/6): 680–91.

Boden, R. (1996), 'Gender and self-employment selection: an empirical assessment', *Journal of Socio-Economics*, 25(6): 671–82.

Bolton, J. E. (1971), *Small firms: Report of the committee of inquiry on small firms*, Cmnd. 4811, London: HMSO.

Bonin, H., A. Constant, K. Tatsiramos and K. F. Zimmermann (2006), 'Ethnic persistence, assimilation and risk proclivity', IZA Discussion Paper no. 2537, Institute for the Study of Labor (IZA).

Bosma, N. and J. Levie (2009), *2009 Global Report*, Global Entrepreneurship Monitor.

Brown, C., J. Hamilton and J. Medoff (1990), *Employers Large and Small*, Cambridge, MA: Harvard University Press.

Brown, S., L. Farrell and M. Harris (2007), 'Who are the self-employed? A new empirical approach', Paper presented at the Work and Pensions Economics Group seminar, October.

Bryson, A. and M. White (1996), *From Unemployment to Self-employment*, Report 820, Policy Studies Institute.

Burke, A. E., F. R. Fitzroy and M. A. Nolan (2000), 'When less is more: distinguishing between entrepreneurial choice and performance', *Oxford Bulletin of Economics and Statistics*, 62(5): 565–87.

Burke, A. E., F. R. Fitzroy and M. A. Nolan (2002), 'Self-employment wealth and job creation: the roles of gender, non-pecuniary motivation and entrepreneurial ability', *Small Business Economics*, 19: 255–70.

Cagetti, M. and M. de Nardi (2006), 'Entrepreneurship, frictions and wealth', *Journal of Political Economy*, 114(5): 835–70.

Cahuc, P. and W. Koeniger (2007), 'Feature: Employment protection legislation', *Economic Journal*, 117(521): 185–8.

Campbell, M. and M. Daly (1992), 'Self-employment: into the 1990s', *Employment Gazette*.

Carrasco, R. (1999), 'Transitions to and from self-employment in Spain: an empirical analysis', *Oxford Bulletin of Economics and Statistics*, 61: 315–41.

Carter, S. (2009), 'The rewards of entrepreneurship: exploring entrepreneurial income, wealth and economic well-being', Working Paper 09–01, Hunter Centre for Entrepreneurship, University of Strathclyde Business School, University of Strathclyde, June.

Casson, M. (2005), 'Entrepreneurship and the theory of the firm', *Journal of Economic Behavior & Organization*, 58: 327–48.

Chell, E., J. M. Haworth and S. Brearley (1991), *The Entrepreneurial Personality: Concepts, cases, and categories*, London and New York: Routledge.

Chittenden, F., H. Foster and B. Sloan (2010), *Taxation and Red Tape: The cost to British business of complying with the UK tax system*, London: Institute of Economic Affairs.

Chittenden, F., S. Kauser and P. Poutziouris (2002), 'Regulatory burdens of small business: a literature review', Project funded by the Small Business Service and supported by the Leverhulme Trust.

Chittenden, F., S. Kauser and P. Poutziouris (2005), 'PAYE-NIC compliance costs, empirical evidence from the UK economy', *International Small Business Journal*, 23(6): 635–56.

Chote, R., P. Johnson and G. Myles (eds) (2011), *Dimensions of Tax Design: The Mirrlees Review*, Research Paper no. 25/2011, Oxford University Press and Oxford Legal Studies.

Clark, K. and S. Drinkwater (2000), 'Pushed in or pulled out? Self-employment among ethnic minorities in England and Wales', *Labour Economics*, 7: 603–28.

Clark, K. and S. Drinkwater (2007a), 'Segregation preferences and labour market outcomes', *Economics Letters*, 94(2): 278–83.

Clark, K. and S. Drinkwater (2007b), 'Ethnic minorities in the labour market: dynamics and diversity', Published for the Joseph Rowntree Foundation by the Policy Press.

Clark, K., S. Drinkwater and D. Leslie (1998), 'Ethnicity and self-employment earnings in Britain 1973–1995', *Applied Economics Letters*, 5: 631–4.

Coase, R. H. (1937), 'The nature of the firm', *Economica* (New Series), 4(16): 386–405.

Constant, A., Y. Shachmurove and K. Zimmermann (2007), 'What makes an entrepreneur and does it pay? Native men, Turks, and other migrants in Germany', *International Migration*, 45(4): 71–100.

Cosh, A. and A. Hughes (eds) (2003), *Enterprise Challenged: Policy and Performance in the British SME Sector 1999–2002*, Cambridge: ESRC Centre for Business Research.

Cowling, M., M. Taylor and P. Mitchell (2004), 'Job creators', *Manchester School*, 72(5): 601–17.

Crawford, C., L. Dearden, A. Mesnard, J. Shaw, B. Sianesi and P. Urwin (2008), 'Estimating ethnic parity in Jobcentre Plus programmes: a quantitative analysis using the Work and Pensions Longitudinal Study (WPLS)', Research Report no. 491, Department for Work and Pensions.

Crawford, C. and J. Freedman (2010), 'Small business taxation', in J. Mirrlees, S. Adam, T. Besley, R. Blundell, S. Bond, R. Chote, M. Gammie, P. Johnson, G. Myles and J. Poterba (eds), *Dimensions of Tax Design: The Mirrlees Review*, Oxford University Press for Institute for Fiscal Studies.

Cressy, R. (2000), 'Credit rationing or entrepreneurial risk aversion? An alternative explanation for the Evans and Jovanovic finding', *Economics Letters*, 66(2): 235–40.

Daunfeldt, S.-O., N. Elert and D. Johansson (2010), 'The economic contribution of high-growth firms: do definitions matter?', Ratio Working Papers no. 151, May.

Davis, S., J. Haltiwanger and S. Schuh (1996a), *Job Creation and Destruction*, Cambridge, MA: MIT Press.

Davis, S., J. Haltiwanger and S. Schuh (1996b), 'Small business and job creation: dissecting the myth and reassessing the facts', *Small Business Economics*, 8: 297–315.

De Wit, G. (1993), 'Models of self-employment in a competitive market', *Journal of Economic Surveys*, 7: 367–97.

Delmar, F., P. Davidsson and W. B. Gartner (2003), 'Arriving at the high-growth firm', *Journal of Business Venturing*, 18(2): 189–216.

Department of Trade and Industry (2007), *Household Survey of Entrepreneurship 2005*, Small Business Service.

Drucker, P. (2007), *Innovation and Entrepreneurship*, Butterworth-Heinemann.

Dunn, T. and D. Holtz-Eakin (2000), 'Financial capital, human capital, and the transition to self-employment: evidence from intergenerational links', *Journal of Labor Economics*, 18(2): 282–305.

Economist (2009), 'A special report on entrepreneurship', 14 March.

Evans, D. and B. Jovanovic (1989), 'An estimated model of entrepreneurial choice under liquidity constraints', *Journal of Political Economy*, 97: 808–27.

Fairlie, R. (2005), 'Entrepreneurship and earnings among young adults from disadvantaged families', *Journal of Small Business Economics*, 25(3): 223–36.

Fletcher, I. (2001), 'A small business perspective on regulation in the UK', *Economic Affairs*, 21(2): 17–22.

Forth, J., H. Bewley and A. Bryson (2006), *Small and Medium Sized Enterprises: Findings from the 2004 Workplace Employment Relations Survey*.

Frank, M. W. (1998), 'Schumpeter on entrepreneurs and innovation: a reappraisal', *Journal of the History of Economic Thought*, 20: 505–16.

Fraser, S. (2005), *Finance for Small and Medium Sized Enterprises: A Report on the 2004 UK Survey of SME Finances*, Coventry: Warwick Business School.

Fraser, S. and F. Greene (2004), 'Are entrepreneurs eternal optimists or do they "get real"?', Centre for Small and Medium Sized Enterprises, Warwick Business School,

Freedman, J. (2001), 'Employed or self-employed? Tax classification of workers and the changing labour market', Discussion paper published by the Tax Law Review Committee and the Institute for Fiscal Studies.

Friedberg, R. M. (2000), 'You can't take it with you? Immigrant assimilation and the portability of human capital', *Journal of Labor Economics*, 18(2): 221–51.

Friedman, M. (1992), 'Do old fallacies ever die?', *Journal of Economic Literature*, 30(4): 2139–42.

Galbraith, J. K. (1956), *American Capitalism: The concept of countervailing power*, Boston, MA: Houghton Mifflin.

Gallup Organisation (2010), *Entrepreneurship in the EU and beyond: analytical report*, Directorate-General for Enterprise and Industry, European Commission.

Georgellis, Y. and H. J. Wall (2000), 'What makes a region entrepreneurial? Evidence from Britain', *Annals of Regional Science*, 34(3): 385–403.

Gomez, R. and E. Santor (2001), 'Membership has its privileges: the effect of social capital and neighbourhood characteristics on the earnings of microfinance borrowers', *Canadian Journal of Economics*, 34: 943–66.

Goss, D. (2005), 'Schumpeter's legacy? Interaction and emotions in the sociology of entrepreneurship', *Entrepreneurship Theory and Practice*, 29(2): 205–18.

Granger, B., J. Stanworth and C. Stanworth (1995), 'Self-employment career dynamics: the case of "unemployment push" in UK book publishing', *Work Employment and Society*, 9(3): 499–516.

Haltiwanger, J., R. Jarmin and J. Miranda (2010), 'Who creates jobs? Small vs. large vs. young', Discussion Paper 101910, Center for Economic Studies (CES), US Census Bureau, August.

Hamilton, B. H. (2000), 'Does entrepreneurship pay? An empirical analysis of the returns of self-employment', *Journal of Political Economy*, 108(3): 604–31.

Harper, D. A. (2003), *Foundations of Entrepreneurship and Economic Development*, New York: Routledge.

Harvey, M. (1995), *Towards the Insecurity Society: The tax trap of self-employment*, London: Institute of Employment Rights.

Harvey, M. (2001), *Undermining Construction*, London: Institute of Employment Rights.

Harvey, M. and F. Behling (2010), 'Self-employment and bogus self-employment in the European construction industry', Project carried out with the financial support of the European Commission.

Hayek, F. A. (1945), 'The use of knowledge in society', *American Economic Review*, 35: 519–30.

Heckman, J. (1998), 'Detecting discrimination', *Journal of Economic Perspectives*, 12(2): 101–16.

Henley, A. (2007), 'Entrepreneurial aspiration and transition into self-employment: evidence from British longitudinal data', *Entrepreneurship and Regional Development*, 19(3): 253–80.

Henrekson, M. and D. Johansson (2010), 'Gazelles as job creators: a survey and interpretation of the evidence', *Small Business Economics*, 35: 227–44.

HM Revenue and Customs and HM Treasury (2009), *False self-employment in construction: taxation of workers*, July, consultation document.

HM Treasury (2002), *Cross Cutting Review of Services for Small Business*, London: HM Treasury.

Holtz-Eakin, D., H. S. Rosen and R. Weathers (2000), 'Horatio Alger meets the mobility tables', *Small Business Economics*, 14(4): 243–74.

Huerta de Soto, J. (2008), *The Austrian School*, Cheltenham: Edward Elgar, in association with the Institute of Economic Affairs.

Institute of Directors (2011), *Regulation Reckoner 2011: counting the real cost of regulation*, IoD Policy Paper.

Jovanovic, B. (1982), 'Selection and the evolution of industry', *Econometrica*, 50(3): 649–70.

Kan, K. and W.-D. Tsai (2006), 'Entrepreneurship and risk aversion', *Small Business Economics*, 26(5): 465–74.

Kihlstrom, R. E. and J.-J. Laffont (1979), 'A general equilibrium entrepreneurial theory of firm formation based on risk aversion', *Journal of Political Economy*, 87(4): 719–49.

Kirzner, I. M. (1985), *Discovery and the Capitalist Process*, Chicago, IL: University of Chicago Press.

Kirzner, I. M. (1997), 'Entrepreneurial discovery and the competitive market process: an Austrian approach', *Journal of Economic Literature*, XXXV: 60–85.

Klepper, S. and E. Graddy (1990), 'The evolution of new industries and the determinants of market structure', *RAND Journal of Economics*, 21: 27–44.

Knight, F. H. (1921), *Risk, Uncertainty and Profit*, Boston, MA: Houghton Mifflin Co.

Kotey, B. (1999), 'Debt financing and factors internal to the business', *International Small Business Journal*, 17(3): 11–29.

Kraft, H., G. Kroisandt and M. Muller (2002), 'Assessing the discriminatory power of credit scores', Discussion paper,

Fraunhofer Institut für Techno- und Wirtschaftsmathematik (ITWM) and Humboldt-Universität zu Berlin.

Lindbeck, A. and D. J. Snower (1988), 'Cooperation, harassment, and involuntary unemployment: an insider-outsider approach', *American Economic Review*, 78(1): 167–88.

Lindsay, C. and C. Macaulay (2004), 'Growth in self-employment in the UK: further investigation into the causes of the increase in self-employment in the UK since 2002', *Labour Market Trends*, 112(10): 399–404.

Lofstrom, M. (2009), 'Does self-employment increase the economic well-being of low-skilled workers?', IZA Discussion Paper no. 4539, Institute for the Study of Labor (IZA).

Marshall, A. (1949 [1920]), *Principles of Economics*, 8th edn, London: Macmillan.

Mason, C. (2011), 'Creating good public policy to support high growth firms', EPRC Seminar.

Meager, N., G. Court and J. Moralee (1996), 'Self-employment and the distribution of income', in J. Hills (ed.), *New Inequalities*, Cambridge: Cambridge University Press.

Mises, L. V. (1949), *Human Action*, New Haven, CT: Yale University Press.

Neal, D. A. and W. R. Johnson (1996), 'The role of premarket factors in black–white wage differences', *Journal of Political Economy*, 104(5): 869–95.

Neumark, D., B. Wall and J. Zhang (2008), 'Do small businesses create more jobs? New evidence for the United States from the National Establishment Time Series', IZA Discussion Paper no. 3888, Institute for the Study of Labor.

Nicoletti, G. and S. Scarpetta (1999), 'Regulation, productivity and growth: OECD evidence', OECD Economics Department Working Papers no. 347.

North, R. (1993), 'Death by regulation: the butchery of the British meat industry', Health Series no. 12, Institute of Economic Affairs.

OECD (Organisation for Economic Co-operation and Development) (2004), *Effective policies for small business: a guide for the policy review process and strategic plans for micro, small and medium enterprises*, UNIDO and OECD.

OECD (Organisation for Economic Co-operation and Development) (2005), *OECD SME and Entrepreneurship Outlook*.

Office for National Statistics (2010), *Business Demography 2009: Enterprise births, deaths and survival*, Statistical Bulletin.

Parker, C. (2004), *The Economics of Self-employment and Entrepreneurship*, Cambridge: Cambridge University Press.

Parker, S. (2007), 'Entrepreneurs, ageing and retirement', Work and Pensions Economics Group Seminar.

Parker, S. C. (2002), 'Do banks ration credit to new enterprises and should governments intervene?', *Scottish Journal of Political Economy*, 49(2): 162–95.

Parker, S. C., Y. Belghitar and T. Barmby (2005), 'Wage uncertainty and the labour supply of self-employed workers', *Economic Journal*, 115(502): C190–C207.

Parnitzke, T. (2005), 'Credit scoring and the sample selection bias', Institute of Insurance Economics, University of St Gallen, Switzerland.

Redston, A. (2004), 'Small business in the eye of the storm', *British Tax Review*, 5: 566–81.

Rees, H. and A. Shah (1986), 'An empirical analysis of self-employment in the UK', *Journal of Applied Econometrics*, 1(1): 95–108.

Reize, F. (2000), 'Leaving unemployment for self-employment: a discrete duration analysis of determinants and stability of self-employment among former unemployed', ZEW Discussion Papers 00–26, Centre for European Economic Research.

Robson, M. (2003), 'Does stricter employment protection legislation promote self-employment?, *Small Business Economics*, 21: 309–19.

Roper, S., N. Driffield, V. Sena, D. Anon-Higon and J. Scott (2006), 'Exploring gender differentials in access to finance – an econometric analysis of survey data', Report prepared for the Small Business Service.

Say, J. B. (1803), *A Treatise on Political Economy*.

Schloss, H. (1968), 'The concept of entrepreneurship in economic development', *Journal of Economic Issues*, 2(2): 228–32.

Schumpeter, J. (1934), *The Theory of Economic Development*, Cambridge, MA: Harvard University Press.

Schumpeter, J. (1937), Preface to the Japanese edn of 'Theorie der Wirtschaftlichen Entwicklung', in J. Schumpeter (1989), *Essays on Entrepreneurs, Innovations, Business Cycles and the Evolution of Capitalism*, ed. R. Clemence, New Brunswick, NJ: Transaction Publishers, pp. 165–8.

Schumpeter, J. (1989), *Essays on Entrepreneurs, Innovations, Business Cycles and the Evolution of Capitalism*, ed. R. Clemence, New Brunswick, NJ: Transaction Publishers.

Shane, S. (2009), 'Why encouraging more people to become entrepreneurs is bad policy', *Small Business Economics*, 33(2): 141–9.

Stangler, D. (2010), 'High-growth firms and the future of the American economy', Kauffman Foundation Research Series on Firm Formation and Economic Growth.

Stanworth, C. and J. Stanworth (1995), 'The self-employed without employees – autonomous or atypical?', *Industrial Relations Journal*, 3.

Stevenson, H. H. and J. C. Jarillo (1990), 'A paradigm of entrepreneurship: entrepreneurial management', *Strategic Management Journal*, 11(5): 17–27.

Taleb, N. N. (2007), *The Black Swan: The Impact of the Highly Improbable*, New York: Random House.

Taylor, M. P. (1996), 'Earnings, independence or unemployment: why become self-employed?', *Oxford Bulletin of Economics and Statistics*, 58: 253–66.

Taylor, M. P. (1999), 'Survival of the fittest: an analysis of self-employment duration in Britain', *Economic Journal*, Vol. 109.

Urwin, P. (2006), 'Age discrimination: legislation and human capital accumulation', *Employee Relations*, 28(1), January.

Urwin, P., M. Gould and L. Page (2010), 'Are there changes in the characteristics of UK Higher Education around the time of the 2006 reforms? Analysis of Higher Education Statistics Agency (HESA) data, 2002/3 to 2007/8', Working Paper 14, Department for Business, Innovation and Skills.

Urwin, P., V. Karuk, F. Buscha and B. Siara (2008a), 'Small businesses in the UK: new perspectives on evidence and policy', Commissioned by the Federation of Small Businesses.

Urwin, P., V. Karuk, P. Hedges and F. Auton (2008b), 'The role of brands in UK economy and society', Commissioned by the British Brands Group.

Urwin, P., C. Stokes and E. Michielsens (2011), 'The removal of employers' ability to specify a Default Retirement Age (DRA): what are the implications for the UK workplace?', Mimeo.

Van Stel, A. and V. Stunnenburg (2004), 'Linking business ownership and perceived economic complexity: an empirical analysis of 18 OECD countries', Discussion Papers on Entrepreneurship, Growth and Public Policy, Max Planck Institute.

Varian, H. R., J. Farrell and C. Shapiro (2007), *The Economics of Information Technology*, Cambridge: Cambridge University Press.

Westhead, P., D. Ucbasaran and M. Wright (2005), 'Experience and cognition: do novice, serial and portfolio entrepreneurs differ?', *International Small Business Journal*, 23(1): 72–98.

Williamson, O. E. (1990), 'Chester Barnard and the incipient science of organization', in O. E. Williamson (ed.), *Organization Theory: From Chester Barnard to the present and beyond*, New York: Oxford University Press, pp. 172–206.

Williamson, O. E. (2002), 'The theory of the firm as governance structure: from choice to contract', *Journal of Economic Perspectives*, 16(3): 171–95.

Williamson, O. E. (2005), 'Transaction cost economics and business administration', *Scandinavian Journal of Management*, 21: 19–40.

ABOUT THE IEA

The Institute is a research and educational charity (No. CC 235 351), limited by guarantee. Its mission is to improve understanding of the fundamental institutions of a free society by analysing and expounding the role of markets in solving economic and social problems.

The IEA achieves its mission by:

- a high-quality publishing programme
- conferences, seminars, lectures and other events
- outreach to school and college students
- brokering media introductions and appearances

The IEA, which was established in 1955 by the late Sir Antony Fisher, is an educational charity, not a political organisation. It is independent of any political party or group and does not carry on activities intended to affect support for any political party or candidate in any election or referendum, or at any other time. It is financed by sales of publications, conference fees and voluntary donations.

In addition to its main series of publications the IEA also publishes a termly journal, *Economic Affairs*.

The IEA is aided in its work by a distinguished international Academic Advisory Council and an eminent panel of Honorary Fellows. Together with other academics, they review prospective IEA publications, their comments being passed on anonymously to authors. All IEA papers are therefore subject to the same rigorous independent refereeing process as used by leading academic journals.

IEA publications enjoy widespread classroom use and course adoptions in schools and universities. They are also sold throughout the world and often translated/reprinted.

Since 1974 the IEA has helped to create a worldwide network of 100 similar institutions in over 70 countries. They are all independent but share the IEA's mission.

Views expressed in the IEA's publications are those of the authors, not those of the Institute (which has no corporate view), its Managing Trustees, Academic Advisory Council members or senior staff.

Members of the Institute's Academic Advisory Council, Honorary Fellows, Trustees and Staff are listed on the following page.

The Institute gratefully acknowledges financial support for its publications programme and other work from a generous benefaction by the late Alec and Beryl Warren.

Other papers recently published by the IEA include:

The Legal Foundations of Free Markets
Edited by Stephen F. Copp
Hobart Paperback 36; ISBN 978 0 255 36591 8; £15.00

Climate Change Policy: Challenging the Activists
Edited by Colin Robinson
Readings 62; ISBN 978 0 255 36595 6; £10.00

Should We Mind the Gap?
Gender Pay Differentials and Public Policy
J. R. Shackleton
Hobart Paper 164; ISBN 978 0 255 36604 5; £10.00

Pension Provision: Government Failure Around the World
Edited by Philip Booth et al.
Readings 63; ISBN 978 0 255 36602 1; £15.00

New Europe's Old Regions
Piotr Zientara
Hobart Paper 165; ISBN 978 0 255 36617 5; £12.50

Central Banking in a Free Society
Tim Congdon
Hobart Paper 166; ISBN 978 0 255 36623 6; £12.50

Verdict on the Crash: Causes and Policy Implications
Edited by Philip Booth
Hobart Paperback 37; ISBN 978 0 255 36635 9; £12.50

The European Institutions as an Interest Group
The Dynamics of Ever-Closer Union
Roland Vaubel
Hobart Paper 167; ISBN 978 0 255 36634 2; £10.00

An Adult Approach to Education
Alison Wolf
Hobart Paper 168; ISBN 978 0 255 36586 4; £10.00

Taxation and Red Tape
The Cost to British Business of Complying with the UK Tax System
Francis Chittenden, Hilary Foster & Brian Sloan
Research Monograph 64; ISBN 978 0 255 36612 0; £12.50

Ludwig von Mises – A Primer
Eamonn Butler
Occasional Paper 143; ISBN 978 0 255 36629 8; £7.50

Does Britain Need a Financial Regulator?
Statutory Regulation, Private Regulation and Financial Markets
Terry Arthur & Philip Booth
Hobart Paper 169; ISBN 978 0 255 36593 2; £12.50

Hayek's *The Constitution of Liberty*
An Account of Its Argument
Eugene F. Miller
Occasional Paper 144; ISBN 978 0 255 36637 3; £12.50

Fair Trade Without the Froth
A Dispassionate Economic Analysis of 'Fair Trade'
Sushil Mohan
Hobart Paper 170; ISBN 978 0 255 36645 8; £10.00

A New Understanding of Poverty
Poverty Measurement and Policy Implications
Kristian Niemietz
Research Monograph 65; ISBN 978 0 255 36638 0; £12.50

The Challenge of Immigration
A Radical Solution
Gary S. Becker
Occasional Paper 145; ISBN 978 0 255 36613 7; £7.50

Sharper Axes, Lower Taxes
Big Steps to a Smaller State
Edited by Philip Booth
Hobart Paperback 38; ISBN 978 0 255 36648 9; £12.50

Other IEA publications

Comprehensive information on other publications and the wider work of the IEA can be found at www.iea.org.uk. To order any publication please see below.

Personal customers

Orders from personal customers should be directed to the IEA:
Clare Rusbridge
IEA
2 Lord North Street
FREEPOST LON10168
London SW1P 3YZ
Tel: 020 7799 8907. Fax: 020 7799 2137
Email: crusbridge@iea.org.uk

Trade customers

All orders from the book trade should be directed to the IEA's distributor:
Gazelle Book Services Ltd (IEA Orders)
FREEPOST RLYS-EAHU-YSCZ
White Cross Mills
Hightown
Lancaster LA1 4XS
Tel: 01524 68765. Fax: 01524 53232
Email: sales@gazellebooks.co.uk

IEA subscriptions

The IEA also offers a subscription service to its publications. For a single annual payment (currently £42.00 in the UK), subscribers receive every monograph the IEA publishes. For more information please contact:
Clare Rusbridge
Subscriptions
IEA
2 Lord North Street
FREEPOST LON10168
London SW1P 3YZ
Tel: 020 7799 8907. Fax: 020 7799 2137
Email: crusbridge@iea.org.uk